D1400710

Rock, Ghost, Willow, Deer

AMERICAN INDIAN LIVES

Editorial Board

General Editor
A. LaVonne Brown Ruoff
University of Illinois at Chicago
(emerita)

Kimberly Blaeser
University of Wisconsin,
Milwaukee

Brenda J. Child
University of Minnesota

R. David Edmunds
University of Texas at Dallas

Clara Sue Kidwell
University of Oklahoma

Daniel F. Littlefield
University of Arkansas

Tsianina Lomawaima
University of Arizona

Gerald Vizenor
University of California,
Berkeley

Rock, Ghost, Willow, Deer

A Story of Survival

Allison Adelle Hedge Coke

University of Nebraska Press

Lincoln & London

© 2004 by
Allison Adelle Hedge Coke
All rights reserved
Manufactured in the
United States of America

⊗

Library of Congress
Cataloging-in-Publication Data
Hedge Coke, Allison.
Rock, ghost, willow, deer : a story of
survival / Allison Adelle Hedge Coke.
p.   cm. — (American Indian lives)
ISBN 0-8032-1527-4 (cloth : alk. paper)
1. Hedge Coke, Allison.   2. Poets,
American—20th century—Biography.
3. Children of schizophrenics—
United States—Biography.   4. Indian
activists—United   States—Biography.
5. College teachers—United States—
Biography.   6. Indian women—
United States—Biography.   7. Indian
poets—United States—Biography.
I. Title.   II. Series.
PS3553.04366 Z474 2004
811'.54—dc22   2003019699

For Travis and Vaughan

What would I be without language?
My existence has been determined
by language, not only the spoken,
but the unspoken, the language
of speech and the language of
motion. I can't remember a world
without memory. Memory,
immediate and far away in the
past, something in the sinew,
blood, ageless cell.

 Simon J. Ortiz,
 The Language We Know

Contents

Illustrations

Acknowledgments

I would like to thank my editor and friend, Gary Dunham, for inspiration, courage, and wonderfully generous support of this work, without which I would be hard-pressed to have arrived here blessed; Wesley Black Elk for friendship and for insisting I write this to begin with; Joy Harjo for continuous support, clarity, intelligence, reason, and for insisting the tangled story here need unfold and fly; Simon Ortiz for commissioning the essay "Seeds for Speaking for the Generations" (University of Arizona Press), from which this book ultimately resulted; the South Dakota Arts Council for a studio grant supporting the work; the MacDowell Colony for a place and time to write the early working draft; David Rivard for suggesting the essay become a book; William Olsen for walking me through the first draft; the honorable Diane Zephier, Betty Holyan, and Heid Erdrich for necessary friendship, sisterhood, and support essential to completion of this book; and David Allan and Jan Evans for a quiet space to write.

This book is dedicated to my granddaughter, Hazel Brianne; babies Lyric and Kyle; my sons, Travis Brent and Timothy Vaughan; the twins Edward and Edwin Two Eagle; my daughter-in-law, Mary Andrews; sister, Pumpkin; adopted sisters, Derya Berti and Kim Shuck; my mom and dad; Aunties Lucy and Nancy; my brother; childhood friends who never betrayed me: Danny Bates, Linda Hammond, Vanessa, JoAnne, and Jo Ann; three lifesavers: Judith Washington, Linda Fizer, and Mr. Noble; and extended family and friends: Diane and Skuya Zephier, Sandy Hinkle, Betty Holyan, Janelle Swallow Price and Tonia, Marsha Stands and Davian, Barbara Dull Knife, Faith and Susan Two Eagle, Crystal Bush, Eleanor Weston, Pte San Tokahe Win Frank, Adam George Two Eagle Jr., Martin, Martina, and Angel.

Acknowledgments

In memory of Derya Berti, Dehl Berti, Cheryl Dunbar, Cangleska Maza, Cousin Richard, my grandmas and grandpas, Aunties Rose and Velma, and all my uncles.

To all of those who walked before me and to those who accompany me on this walk; to those who can't forget and to those who lost remembering; to all those tabooed children of village crazies still among us getting by and to those we lost along the way.

Memory is what compels us to act in the world. It is a deep, though subjective, matter that influences perspective and demeanor. Like fingerprints, no two are alike, yet truth inherently lies somewhere within. And congenital memory, that of belonging by nature to landscapes, runs the deepest of all the rivers of the earth. This memoir is of my memory and is my search for truth in self and in the world surrounding me for the first thirty years here. Some names have been changed to provide for anonymity where appropriate.

Rock, Ghost, Willow, Deer

1

Of Seeds

I descend from mobile and village peoples, interracial, ingenious, adventurous, and bold. None famous, none of any more than humble means, though in this great ancestral river thoroughly bloodstreamed true, I am born from those so devoted to their beliefs and way of living they would eagerly choose to be memorialized through songs or stories of honorable doings, or maybe through sharing a bit of tobacco on special occasions, rather than by accumulating material legacies in life.

Before me and around me were warriors, fighters, hunters, fishers, gatherers, growers, traders, midwives, runners, avid horse people, weavers, seamstresses, artists, craftspeople, musicians, storytellers, singers, linguists, dreamers, philosophers; they were Huron, Tsa la gi (Cherokee), Muscogee, French-Canadian, Portuguese, English, Alsace-Lorraine, Irish, Welsh; and there was the insane.

I understood all of this by the age of three.

When I was a tiny child, my father would sit me up at the hardwood kitchen table near my older sister, Pumpkin, and give us seed and pony beads to string. I could barely reach the surface of what seemed then to be an enormous gate-leg table to work, so I propped myself up higher by sitting with my feet and knees tucked under me on the light-brown vinyl chair seat. Being included made me feel like a big girl, so I worked hard.

As I remember, this table was off to the side of our kitchen on the north side of the house. We lived on an unfinished road, speckled with small clusters of mixed-blood and Indian families, on East Eleventh Street in Amarillo, Texas. My family had settled there temporarily because of my father's work in the Department of Agriculture. Amarillo is supposed to be a dry place, but when I was young, sometimes in spring, the smell of rain would hang in the air for days. Mint lined our front porch; a mud puppy we called Sam and a box turtle the size of a small shaker lived under it. The grasshoppers were so fat back then we would hull them out and eat their meat for snacks, imitating my father's Depression stories, just to make an impression on other kids.

I was born August 4, 1958, just north of the area. Named Allison Adele, my first name acknowledging a character in a book who, though slightly crippled herself, helped people who had special needs, the second honoring my mother's aunt Ivy Adele. I was told that the two names together mean "back foot soldier (rear or tail fighter) for truth (honor)." My birth certificate reads "Hedge Coke," as two words, and that is how I spell my last name. My sister's certificate reads "Hedge-coke" as one word. It varies throughout my family. My father says the name was closer to Crow (male), or Bird in the Bush, or Bush Crow originally, and we think of it in that way today still. I have other names, but they are personal—mostly unspoken. All my names are good names, and I am thankful for them. A name creates life patterns, which form and shape a life; my life, like my name, must have been formed many times over then handed to me to realize.

My dad has a good sense of humor, so when the nicknames come, they are from him. My toddler nickname was Baby No. The movie *Doctor No* was released locally while I was beginning to get mobile. I was into everything. My dad says he couldn't resist. He calls my sister Pumpkin Head since her face is round and full. She smiles wide, too. These are the first names we knew each other by. We see Baby No and Pumpkin Head in each other's eyes still today.

In that kitchen my first clear memories begin. We are surrounded by cabinets, far above my reach, filled partially with flour, cornmeal, cereal, and macaroni and cheese, just as in every other house nearby. The windows are all open. Crossing the ceiling corners are cobwebs that my father saves for blood coagulants in case we get cut or step on nails barefoot. If a spider happens out onto the linoleum floor, he scoops it up with his bare hands and carries it outside, allowing it to be free to make webs elsewhere. He says the spider brought both pottery and weaving to The People and we should respect her for doing so.

Each time my father starts us beading, I try my best to get my stubby fingers to shape long, bright necklaces with corn and flower patterns. He sits across from us and works on nine- and twelve-row patterns of his own. I am still young enough to be limited to stringing ponies; I finish a pattern that actually resembles my intention. My father looks it over carefully, nods, and, without saying anything about the beadwork, smiles and says my face is beaming.

I ask him what a beam is, and he tells me it is the stroke of sunlight pouring through a clearing in the clouds.

I didn't know my face could do such a thing.

While we were busy working on the beadwork, my father would tell us about our ancestors and relatives, about their joys, struggles, and great and terrible survivals. I loved his stories so much I taught myself to read by the time I was four, so I would never be without stories. My father's voice was gentle and strong, rhythmically patterned, like a song, somehow making it easy to remember things he said. The ancestors we came from seemed to me like beads strung together, patterned, woven into a whole people. Even the old heart beads, one color layered over another, represented individuals with more than one side or purpose in life. And what he didn't say—details about certain character traits and personal losses—was carried across to us by a raised eyebrow or sad expression on his deep brown face. This outright avoidance was just as important to our education as what he did say out loud. Maybe even more so.

At the kitchen table, we learned about our universe, our world, and ourselves, about being Cherokee, Real People, relatives of deer, and carriers of an Eternal Flame. We heard stories of our beautiful home in North Carolina and how this home full of gorgeous mountains, hills, valleys, rivers, and streams also spread throughout what is now Tennessee, Georgia, South Carolina, Virginia, and other surrounding areas in the southeastern United States. This land had life and spirit just as we do. My father told stories of deer, otter, bear, and birds; of corn, squash, beans, and berries; of ball games and Little People; of sky vault and the world beneath the water.

He talked of this great earth—the Great Smoky Mountains, the Appalachians, the land of the Blue Ridge (Oconoluftee)—and the many mountains and peaks physically marking our occurrence in the world. These were the lands of birth for First Man and Corn Mother, the lands Buzzard had created with a great flapping about of his wings in mud, and the lands of the great flood where a dog talked and saved man. Pumpkin and I heard of the greatness of the stars and the Dog Road to the Darkening Land. We learned of the rivers and streams where people exchanged clothes and made relations, of dance squares where celebrations took place to honor the seasons and life, of the mighty and many mounds my ancestors built for burial and prayer during a priesthood that sprang forth from the people and ended by the people's hands, where the ghosts were so strong that they even drove off enemy troops during the Civil War. My father recounted tales of rich black soil and luxuriant flora greening the topsoil quilled with lavish tree trunks and topped with a canopy of leaves and pine needles thickly spread about all over this great place we originated from. The bones of our Cherokee people furnished this soil with nutrients and fertilized all that we reaped from its bounty. We were as cyclic as the phases of the sun and the moon, as sequential as time.

We learned of the evils of Andrew Jackson, of his troops rendering grease from Indian captives they killed to cook their meats in, and of his all-out hatred for and forced removal of our people. We learned of the wretched Georgian settlers released from English prisons to take away our home, who sought the riches of our mountains and forced us away. Dad told us about some of our ancestors hiding out and remaining forever in the heart of the Smoky Mountains and never leaving, of how a man named Tsa li gave himself up to American troops so that those of us in hiding might remain where we had lived. The People were forcibly removed to Indian Territory (present Oklahoma) by these troops, with some four or five thousand people dying on the way—like our own Grandma Bessie Walker snatched away from us and passing away walking—on this Trail Where They Cried. Some other ancestors moved into Arkansas and the Red River area of Texas to avoid the forced internment onto reservations. We had ancestors on this paternal side of the family who followed all these different paths simultaneously. Divided. My father said his own dad, our Grandpa Vaughan (born in 1878), refused tribal enrollment for himself and his children, protesting the "evils of the Removal" and the ruins of the "diabolical Dawe's Act." Grandpa Vaughan stated flatly he wasn't going to be anyone's "PET INDIAN."

We also were taught about being Huron, the other part of my father's Native heritage. Pumpkin and I learned of ancestral lives in bark lodges and long-house villages, of the birch bark canoe peoples from Canada with all its seasonal glory. We were enchanted by stories of long winters and crisp air, of tree sap running, becoming sugars and sweets, of masks cut from live wood and worn for special occasion and purpose, and of the richness of these northeastern lands and the bounty they generously gave our people. Great trees sheltered the lands and the lives of our Huron ancestors entwined with woods and water. The waterways were roads to travel and trade upon; we never left the banks of the woodlands far behind when canoeing. The water was full of mystery and healing properties, and there was great advantage to fighting near the water's edge. My sister and I came to understand the significance of wind and the turtle and the importance of physically interweaving and lacing the edge of the wood line when hunting to appear without notice. My father went on to tell us about the immense abilities of the linguists among our direct Huron ancestors and the mingling of French traders and trappers who saw our grandmothers and fell in love. We learned of secret dreamers and storytellers in our grandma's family.

Pumpkin and I heard how our Huron relations traveled with their French-Canadian men south for many years, following the great wars of the north, where Englishmen and Americans took scalps and skins off of bodies of captive Indian people and cured them for leggings and decorations of the frontiersmen. Our Huron/French-Canadian grandmas and grandpas traded and traveled by canoe and by foot, smoking tobacco to chase away hunger, finally ending up in Indian Territory as well. Our grandmother, Maria Louise, eventually met and married Grandpa Vaughan in a place so many miles from the original Eastern Woodlands homeland of both sides of the family.

My father spoke many times of Granny, Maria Louise (born in 1882). Grandfather Vaughan had passed on from emphysema ten years before I was born, and Granny had joined her husband while I was a couple of months on the way, so I never saw my first grandmother. Pumpkin, the older one, remembered Granny and had similarly colored hair, dark with one spot of red in it. She would grab my hands and show me how Granny danced with her before I was born, adding excited affirmations of how "great" Granny was. For me Granny was story, and story was part of everything I knew.

She was a traditional midwife, bringing hundreds of children into the world for many, many families. Granny was a strong woman who knew all the plants for midwifery and for curing common sicknesses. My father used to make us teas from some of those plants when we were young. He sang children's songs for us, in Indian, that she had sung to him when he was little. Granny continued to help and heal even after she was gone. Once my father dreamed of her pointing toward me as I lay in my crib, her hair long and unbraided. He told us that he awoke suddenly with a feeling of electricity running through him and suddenly found himself in our room. I had suffered an asthma attack and had become still. Even though I wasn't breathing, he had woken up in time for him and my mother to bring me back to life.

We learned from Granny's example what was expected of girls and women. Bringing children into the world was important and should be honored. Once a woman had children of her own it gave her standing among the people as a mother, just as bravery or an important action would give her additional status. Traditionally, our father said, all children would typically stay with the mother until they were past early childhood.

Women's natures developed character early on. We girls were told to be strong—"steadfast like a stone if need be." My father told us girls to be careful how we moved (used) our hands when we were angry because we were "our grandmother's girls" and that anger, while useful for appropriate situations, also was dangerous. We should never be vengeful, no matter how we were treated by anybody; unfounded or unnecessary bad thoughts and wishes, as well as needless violence, are no good. Bold fierceness, though, is proper and justified when defending what is good in the world, what is innocent, pure—life and justice. Pumpkin and I would sometimes marvel at our pudgy little hands after hearing our dad tell us about Granny. We wondered just what they were capable of that we should be careful with them.

At the kitchen table, my sister and I also became aware of my mother's family. Our maternal grandpa, Herbert, was mixed-blood himself. His Portuguese grandfather (an Enos) had been shanghaied in the Mediterranean by Spaniards and narrowly escaped a life of slavery by jumping boat near New York City. This Portuguese grandpa married in with people (Muscogee) in Missouri, and together they migrated back and forth into Canada, their offspring eventually marrying and settling from Minnesota to Alberta, at the base of the Rockies. We also heard stories of his daughter, who gave birth to my mother's father near the shoreline of the Big Stone Lake on the border of what would later become Minnesota and South Dakota. There is Alsace-Lorraine and bits and drops of other European blood in this line as well. My father explained that our maternal grandmother, Sabina (nicknamed Sybil), felt it important to abrogate her husband's lineage in order to flaunt her supposed all-English heritage. She had arrived here as a girl around 1912. One of her English ancestors apparently had no history noted before arriving through Ireland to marry into her family. The name scrawled on his picture was Butcher; he looked very Chinese to us (though we understood clearly we were never to share that opinion with Sabina). Our grandmother had been born and raised in Nottingham and had played in Sherwood Forest; Dad related all he knew of Robin Hood and of the Knights of the Round Table.

Although our father tried his best to engage us in my mother's family, we never felt the same intensity and depth of connection with her ancestors and relatives. This grandma treated us like strangers, and we felt the same about her and her people. And she had allowed our mother to be sent away to boarding school at age five (where we were told she became a prodigy in classic piano). Dad explained that Grandmother Sabina's ancestors were from the same people who had colonized a great part of the hemisphere. Huron fought the Brits, though Cherokee at one time preferred Brits to Americans due to the Brits' acknowledging us as sovereign people, but the colonization had caused long-term hardship and grief for The People—our people.

My father raised us to believe being Indian was what made us who we are—what *shaped* us. We were proud of our ancestors. No matter if we were mixed-blood—we were from people who lived with purpose, with humbleness and personal integrity; and proud we were from truly independent people who had not compromised. The events in my father's stories seemed only a separate part of the same day of the telling. We believed there was no real separation between our lives and those of our ancestors. We knew we would always belong to the wet, green, Eastern Woodlands. We also knew we were travelers, nomadic peoples resulting from and adapting to changes of life upon the earth.

Our paternal aunties and uncles were great sources of story as well. We visited all our extended family, and some of them came to visit us when I was very small. Mom got sick when I was a baby, and when Mom was sick we would sometimes live with these relatives. Velma, Willis, Sid, Sam, John, Tom, Lucy, and Rose were my dad's siblings. It was fascinating to spend so much time with them because of their creative minds and creating hands—all of my father's brothers and sisters were good singers or musicians and were artistic in some way.

Velma, a storyteller and seamstress, was the oldest; born in 1902, she was twenty years older than Dad (amazing to us because we believed Dad to be the oldest father anyone our age had ever known). We particularly loved Auntie Velma. She knew all kinds of stories, how to garden, and how to make all kinds of things, including good food. Everyone loved her fresh bread and soup, mincemeat and raisin pie, and hand-wrung chicken stew with rice simmering in blue-speckled pots and pans. And, of course, she always had a big pot of coffee on the stove for guests and family. She was like a grandma for us kids, a hero, and I liked visiting with older women when I was young. They knew everything.

Velma had an old-woman voice and deep-set lines in her skin to go along with it. Her hair was always pulled back, and she mostly wore cotton print dresses. Though she was a small woman, her lap always proved soft, a feeling of comfort and safety surrounding us whenever we were near her, with breezes sweeping through her open house like soft invitations waiting outdoors. When we went outside with my auntie, she would show us wild plants and foods we could eat. Everyone loved her. She was absolutely my favorite person in the world.

Auntie Velma used to sit us tiny kids up on her lap and tell us funny stories about our family and animals and scary stories of ghosts bothering people. She always told us to listen carefully and would laugh out loud if one of us got too involved in the story and questioned her about it afterward. All my cousins would gather around her. Velma told us that when she wanted us to give her company she would spend time thinking it and we would all come.

Uncle Willis would share with anyone who would listen his expert knowledge on carving, woodworking, rocks, rivers, and earth. His place was surrounded by every kind of rock that could be found within a hundred miles and by wood he had carved or built things with. Sid, John, and Tom were excellent craftsmen. Sid lived off in Colorado, where the family had for decades migrated from Oklahoma, Arkansas, and Texas following the iron rail and crop work during my father's youth. My uncle John was the easy-going, knowledgeable uncle whom my dad favored closely. Tom was known mostly by letters since he had moved far away to the Pacific Northwest and rarely came down to visit, but his letters were welcoming and generous. Lucy was an expert horsewoman and World War II pilot. The lightest complexioned sibling, she was born less than twenty years after the turn of the century, three months premature. My father's childhood hero, Lucy—by her competence, deeds, and fairness—established herself as the authority among the children. Rose painted and wrote poetry. She settled in Oklahoma, having left North Carolina because of racial tensions.

Sam and my father had strained relations. We could feel the tension—sinewy, like tendons ready to snap. This uncle was naturally suspect to us because of my father's feelings. Dad admitted that Sam had once taken him, Rose, and Lucy down into a Plains town (Kim, Colorado) on a wagon, in 1923 or 1924, tied a sign to them, and tried to sell them for "CHEAP INDIAN LABOR." He later tried to trade Auntie Rose for a button hook, and he beat my father regularly while he was growing up. At Sam's place (which we saw only once), he made beautiful silver and stone jewelry and handcrafted musical instruments, so his cabin was filled with the beauty of his handiwork, the scent of fresh wood, stain, and rosin, and tones as soulful as you would expect from the Cherokee talent we were raised to know.

From my aunties and uncles, I began to piece together a picture of my father. As a child in school, following a bedridden year of the terrible rheumatic fever, he had ridden the bus for miles upon the then typical long, uncomfortable wooden benches for seats, and his teachers beat his hands so badly he developed early childhood arthritis. Later my father followed his older sister Lucy's lead and put himself through college. He rode fence, worked as a janitor, and later used a GI Bill he earned from infantry service in World War II to pay his way. He started out by earning a bachelor of science degree in chemistry, worked a couple of years for Phillips Oil Company (then headed by a prominent Tsa la gi man from Oklahoma), but switched to physical therapy training during the polio epidemic before we were born. He ended up working as a physical therapist in Grand Forks, where he enrolled in medical school for a short time. He left North Dakota married to my mother (already a war widow at this time) to work as a physical therapist at Northwest Texas Hospital. After the epidemic was over, he worked a few years as a chemist for the Department of Agriculture, which brought us into the panhandle of Texas for his work. He and Lucy were the first people in our entire paternal family to ever obtain a higher education and to earn bachelor's degrees.

We were proud our father fought in World War II in the South Pacific. He was engaged to a Cheyenne girl when he left for the war, taking off for the fighting with her brother, Russell Fisher. He made friends with other Native people (rather than the other army guys) because there was common ground between them. When in the Philippines, my father noticed the Filipinos were more like Indians than whites. One time he made friends with a Filipino native, who invited him to eat at his hut. A dog loose in the man's yard became supper by nightfall. My father would laugh and admit that Filipino dog tasted pretty good.

Though he never spoke about it much, these war stories also had special impact upon us. His old uniform still hung in the bedroom closet, and we used his military helmets to play in hailstorms, lying in ditches and pretending we were being shelled. My sister was in school at this time, and in those days they spent some school time practicing for air raids and such, so she didn't like to play war as much as my younger brother and I did.

One of Dad's strongest philosophies was his opposition to alcohol of any kind. He always told us never to drink, believing it dulled people and made them inhumane. Being mixed Huron and Cherokee meant that we were of The Real People, and to be real people meant being humane. He spoke openly and honestly about these things to us so that we understood his beliefs and reason. To use alcohol risked this humanity; it was difficult enough to be humane in an often inhumane modern world. Unlike some of the surrounding community, my father's family didn't drink. He claimed that most Indians didn't have the same congenital tolerance to alcohol as Europeans and Asians did because it hadn't always been available. Though he never criticized people who drank, he was very strongly opposed to our using alcohol of any kind.

I don't remember my father ever laying a hand on me during discipline. He didn't have to. Pumpkin and I respected him enough to respond to what he told us, and I knew what he expected of me.

Surrounded by stories, we learned to tell them ourselves. When we were small, my sister and I wrote little stories to each other in letters and pictures with small chunks of Sheetrock on the concrete slab outside our front porch. Because she was a few years older than me, Pumpkin knew more letters and words, so she taught me some of what she knew and I improvised the rest. Sometimes we would draw in dirt with sticks or use burned matches or coal to make black and gray pictures. My sister often mixed together food colors and other stuff from under the kitchen sink to make colors for our pictures.

I remember drawing symbols to represent my sister, my family, and me. All across the cracked up concrete step I drew birds hiding in bushes and clouds dripping with rain. We might stay outside drawing like this the whole day through. Sometimes we talked; sometimes we just let the pictures talk for us. I always placed the sun, flowers, and corn in these pictures, imitating designs we learned stringing beads with my father. These things spoke to me because I understood something about their properties. We created pictures mostly working off of what we knew of our family before, drawing on the stories my father took great amounts of time to tell.

True to our heredity, we did not stay in Amarillo an entire year through. We were always traveling, visiting relatives, following our Indian bloods—Cherokee, Creek, Huron—continually heading back north through Oklahoma, up the CanAm Highway across the Great Plains, and into our cherished Canada, the lands of my father's mother's people and where my mother's family had settled. Wherever we traveled or dwelled, we lived mostly on macaroni, bologna, bread, soup and always on prayer, story, and song. We prayed to greet each morning and to protect us through the night. We sang whenever the feeling moved us. And my father raised us with attention to story as a simple daily ritual, as regular as changing clothes or brushing hair. While I was still young, middle school age, we eventually moved back east to the western North Carolina home of Dad's Tsa la gi people, never to return to Amarillo again.

We were told long ago some young sisters out picking berries heard voices on the winds from the sacred Nuñ ne hi. They warned the girls that a strange people was coming and everything would be different and they would not be so happy in these lands through the changes brought on by the intruders. These voices stayed on winds for some time and instructed Tsa la gi people to join together to fast for seven days so that they might join them in their dwelling places below the mountains and waters so that they might survive the newly approaching strange peoples coming to the lands from the east.

Now at this time no one had seen a live white man, only a skeleton and deceased body, but they knew if the Nuñ ne hi spoke this enemy would come. Peoples in two towns were so pure of heart and mind they listened to everything the spirits told them and believed, so they gathered together in the long houses of two villages to follow the words of the spirits and fasted, sang, and prayed.

The first village peoples were together fasting in a lodge on the seventh day when the Immortals came and lifted the house and its mound to be carried away. The people yelled out in their awe and caused the Immortals to drop the mound; then they collected themselves to rescue the house remaining and lifted it high to the top of Lone Peak, where great forces turned the house to stone after making its inhabitants invisible and immortal to spare them from enduring terrible changes in the world. The stone lodge may still be seen today on that mountain in the Appalachians.

The second village was taken to live in eternal happiness under the waters and remains there immortal. And all Tsa la gi yi know that the true test of faith lies in willingness to sacrifice for a belief, for loyalty for the Great Ones, and for loyalty and reliability among and between people.

2

From Winds

My father's remarkable commitment to telling about our past surrounded us with stories, real, meaningful tales of identity that gathered us up like strands in our paternal grandmother's handmade rag rugs, pulling and binding us together so it was difficult to unravel us even when we stepped out alone. We were fibers in the fabric where we came from—an Indian family, intertribal, mixed-blood, whose parents were educated yet still maintained old-way beliefs and values, who believed in ghosts but were practical minded, and who worked hard and adjusted to whatever came our way. Our family stayed with many relatives, but because we always knew our true place, through Cherokee blood in North Carolina, through Huron blood in Canada, we began to think of ourselves as rocks in a stream of strangler moss. Unflinching. The fluidity in our lives and makeup did not undermine our commitment to principles in a world of clutter. Sometimes rocks dislodge and crack against each other in watery currents, yet they always ascertain certain footing, lodge, and stay put, and this certainty was among us as well.

Yet those rocks of certainty were terribly tested during my childhood by the gale force of my mother's insanity.

My sister, brother, and I shared a bedroom together. Pumpkin slept against the east wall in a separate bed with an attached maple bookcase headboard, while my brother, younger than me by only fifteen months, slept on the bottom bunk under where I slept against the north wall. The bed covers were plaid-printed cotton, and we each had our own pillow. One of my first memories in this room was watching two boats float across my brother's bunk bed. They were small, like wooden or bark toys, and moved along as if the spreads were fluid. They enraptured me, and I told Pumpkin and her friend Trudy, who were in the room with me, but they laughed and said it was my imagination. I had heard about this because my sister had an imaginary friend: a giant rabbit she would feed and talk to. Sometimes I thought I saw grass moving next to her feet in the yard where the rabbit was supposed to be.

I often dreamed I was a deer fawn, and my dreams were filled with lush green clearings and trees filled with ripe fruits. Late in the night Mom would come in, snapping our sleep like a bear through winter-cold branches, the fawn fading far away. We were awoke, late night, to be "informed" about Mom's life and "knowledge" that she passionately described in detail. And, being Canadian, most everything she said ended with "aaayee" or "eh." She told us of their first three babies dying and how one, a boy, was shaped identically to me, his back long and lean, his face light complexioned, his infant bones angular and slim, eh. She told us that the "Buggers" made her lose them and that the American Medical Association was involved in a plot against her.

At night the moonlight brightened our bedroom walls as Mom told stories about ghosts she'd seen when she was young, like the ghosts she watched as a boarding student in Montreal. She said she had witnessed two ghosts, a male and a female, dressed in old-style clothes, go down a basement staircase, where my mother was washing clothes in a Bendix washer. She said the female whispered to her companion, "We should drink some tea." Soon they vanished, and my mother finished her laundry.

My mother loved to tell me a story about a face that peered at her when she was a young child. The face was huge and serene and "nothing to be afraid of," she said. "It was the most intelligent" and "was hard to describe its intelligence it was so obviously great." Mom said she ducked under the covers and reemerged to find it gone. She told us she sometimes prayed to it. I envisioned her preschool age, dressed in cotton slips, with her dark hair twisting down her back. I felt a great empathy toward her because she seemed unable to prevent herself from sharing these stories. It seemed as though something propelled her. Her stories were almost a plea for confirmation.

She said another face once appeared to her while she was attending McGill University. She was rooming on the top floor of a three-story apartment house. The floors were wooden, and she told me she had to wax them on her hands and knees with balls of steel wool. One evening, in a soft light by the closet door, she saw the shape of a face in three parts, "in a smear—like a cloud." She said she got up and turned on the light and the face wasn't there. She turned it off and it was. On again and it was gone. Off again and it was there. She said she thought to herself, "At least it's friendly, eh," and went to bed.

Her madness distorted her voice, so the stories she told had an added inflection of urgency and madness and were scary when she told them, even if she said they were nothing to be afraid of. Afterward, she moved down the hall, continuing her monologue to the Buggers. I wouldn't be able to sleep for hours and hours, waiting in the night for the faces to come peer at us.

My mother held a degree in physiotherapy from McGill University (literally one of the first people in the world to be trained as such and one of the first to work with the polio epidemic, successfully urging my father to join her in her work in North Dakota) and a teaching degree from the Royal Schools of London (Toronto) in classical piano (she was the youngest to ever receive the degree at that time). She suffered from schizophrenia, severe, paranoid delusions, although we were too young to understand at first much about her illness. Furthermore, my mother was afflicted with a terrible thyroid problem, burdening her with strange cravings and a readiness to prepare surrealistic meals. She would, for instance, at times sit down and eat a stick of butter (which she called oleo back then) as if it were a cut of fine meat.

In appearance my mother was modest and proper, always wearing long skirts or pants and no makeup except red lipstick on special occasions. Even in her forties, her face was lined and deeply creased, framed by black hair cropped above the shoulders. Her thick black hair, however, was interrupted by shoots of even thicker stark-white hair—resulting from shock treatments—that would subsequently fall out.

My mother was truly tortured; with great difficulty she struggled with daily life. As an adult my mother heard voices. In a schizophrenically distorted voice inflected with urgency and madness, she ranted about crimes committed by the federal government, churches, and other organized religions (most of which turned out to be somewhat true) and how these agencies were torturing and controlling her through computer programming, bugging devices, and radio waves. The Buggers were "plotting" against her; they could see her, so my mother refused to remove her underclothing when bathing; they bugged the stove ventilation hood in the kitchen; the Buggers were in my parents' bedroom closet—everywhere.

Face and limb muscles twitching, eyes filled with horror and fury, every atom of her being would come alive while screaming at the ventilation hood, "LEAVE me A-lone! Quit RAP-ing ME with RA-dio waves! Leave our FAM-ily a-LONE!" My mother ranted at the bedroom closet whenever we kids took turns bathing or brushing our teeth. We came to believe that great monsters and ghosts lived in that closet and would come torture us too if they noticed us moving about. Afraid to flush the bathroom toilet at night for fear of arousing these beasts, we would flush it with an outstretched foot while a hand was turning the doorknob, prepared to run for the cover and safety of our shared room. I found courage to face that fear one time in the fall of 1961. My mother was crying and screaming at the closet so loudly that I stood on the bed behind her, made myself as fierce looking as possible, and demanded, "LEAVE MY MOTHER ALONE." When nothing happened, I began to realize that the problem lurked not within those walls. I asked Pumpkin later that day, "Do any of the other moms do this?"

Looking into my eyes—thoroughly, completely, and without leaving room for misunderstanding—Pumpkin said quietly, "No. None of them."

My mother spent time in at least three different asylums during our school years—Underwood, the Pavilion, and Dorthea Dix—but her behavior didn't really change dramatically between treatments. She would return home completely blanked out with no memory of anything before that particular date on the calendar, even who we were. In time, she would remember her war with the Buggers, the conflict escalating until she had to go back again. Any trigger could send her back, anytime or anywhere. We were always waiting for the next episode and the next leaving.

The laws for child welfare were anti–birth family pre-1969 and the new welfare acts. In the early 1960s social services thought that when our mother was institutionalized we should be taken away. They said that, because my dad worked, they didn't see how he could possibly raise us. We knew it was simply because he was male, and we could not understand why they couldn't see he already was our father and our mother, the only stable parent we had. When Mom was home, they certainly never called. They thought that everything was fine as long as there was a "mother" in the home.

My dad placed us with his relatives when they threatened to take us away from him. We had an uncle we stayed with a few times. He lived a day's travel away, in Seibert, a town with grain elevators, above the general store in a flat apartment. The three of us were given our own room together, and we could watch people in the store below through a grate in the floor near their dining table. We would lay our faces on the grate watching customers shop until our skin was branded with the grate's metalwork. My uncle and his wife barely spoke to us; most of our older relatives were people of few words, but they fed us well. I was just under three, but I vividly remember my father placing a postcard of what would soon be called a Palomino horse in my hand, and I remember holding onto the postcard or having it tucked some-where in my clothing almost always. I remember I thought it was my only link to him when he left.

Living on mostly macaroni and cheese at home, we weren't famil-iar with all the kinds of food they ate there in eastern Colorado. We were afraid to even try most of it. We were housed well enough, and it was warm in the apartment above the store, but we knew we were there because we were tabooed, because of insanity, because of the law. We never spoke to anyone in that town except our uncle and his wife. Their kids were older and grown by this time, and they were pretty much alone. Pumpkin told me that it was okeh because our cousin Bub was left at Velma's before, she thought, because his own mom, our first cousin, drank, and we all thought the world of him still, so we believed the taboo would be short lived.

While we were there, my uncle John and his wife, Julia, came to visit us, and I ran away because he looked so much like my dad, only older, thinking maybe Uncle John was my dad's ghost or that someone had done something incredible to my dad that aged him.

We "visited" many of our dad's relatives during grade school. I was always afraid of what someone could do to my parents while I was separated from them. It certainly seemed an issue. The taboo on us never dwindled, and we felt the strange dissonance of it always.

When she would return home, my mother's insanity weighed incredibly upon us all. My mother hardly required sleep, and almost all the time while awake she contended with the Buggers so loudly that if we were playing with kids a mile away, and if the wind was right, we could hear her. Many in our community were deeply involved with alcohol, so we heard screaming from other houses too. But our situation was different—the outbursts occurred continuously without someone grabbing a bottle or can. Because trouble was more predictable at our neighbors, the alcoholic houses actually became refuge for us as we were growing up (until those steadily drinking neighbors would have mood changes and begin to fight among themselves or beat up on their kids). The parents who drank were up as late at night as we were, and I could stay visiting till way after Johnny Carson was over and no one would ever notice. Then, walking home alone, and having heard words like "perpetrator" since I was an infant, it was easy to imagine someone would most certainly jump me, sight unseen, from the many honeysuckle bushes growing along the way. It never truly happened this way—no one ever jumped from the surrounding shrubbery, but the thought alone invoked split-second possible perpetrator sightings, which thoroughly scared me and made me run. Most of the nondrinking families seemed to regard my mother's insanity as contagious and wouldn't let us in their yards.

We were once invited to a house where no one was sick or drinking. It was for a birthday party for some distant relatives who had oil on their Oklahoma and Texas panhandle lands. They even sent invitations with two gray tabby kittens sitting at a white table sipping soda through straws. When you pulled the card open, it unfolded a long table full of more kittens in between them at a party.

It is the only invitation I remember seeing as a child.

It was late summer; the party kids were dressed up in store-bought clothes, all frilly and proper. Pumpkin and I were in our favorite broadcloth shifts my dad had made for us. I hated shoes, and since we only got one pair a year, mine were always for running or playing ball and did not go at all with dresses, so I was soon barefoot, and Pumpkin had on some worn canvas sneakers while the other girls there had on patent-leather shoes. They made fun of us and pointed at us, wrinkling up their noses.

I remember that my sister had given the girl a Chatty Cathy doll we purchased with S & H Greenstamps. Pumpkin had many nonspeaking dolls, and she really wanted this one or at least to play with it. The little girl had stacks and stacks of presents lying on a wooden table strewn with colored paper and bows. So Pumpkin ventured a polite request to play with the doll for a little while. The girl wouldn't let her, and my sister turned to me and, without moving her lips, said, "do it now!" The next thing I remember we seemed to be floating high above the party and the properly dressed girls, and we were free. Pumpkin still looked at me and talked to me without words coming from her mouth, and she said, "If they knew we could do this they wouldn't make fun of us, Ali."

I don't exactly remember what truly happened when she commanded me. Though, I distinctly remember the feeling—the spaciousness. I remember what everything looked like below us, children twirling around the birthday girl amid presents and paper and Pumpkin's face, particularly her eyes, which seemed to speak for her, though I heard her voice in my mind as if she spoke. I remember clearly where we were, suddenly high in the air. Then someone far below yelled that there was cake to eat, and we zipped back down to join in. It is a strange memory. As an adult I once asked my sister about this memory, and she remembered some of it but not all, and we spoke of our childhood imaginations, and my dad still remembers taking us there to the party and dropping us off. I do not claim to understand this memory, but for me it is as if it happened a few moments ago.

At our home, we had our own version of festivities. Mom would stay up all night warring with the walls. Then sometime, during the middle of the day, she would nap to recharge. Covered up with my paternal grandmother's handwoven rag rugs, she'd lie on the "divan" underneath watercolor paintings her mother painted of the

Rockies. Of course, we were supposed to sleep at the same time. She would put us in our room and tell us to stay there. Pumpkin, being the oldest, instructed my brother and me to wait until Mom was sleeping, then climb over the wooden child's gate hinged at our bedroom door. Then we went to the kitchen and climbed cabinet shelves like stairs to reach Nestle's Quik mixture to make drinks from milk. We'd often had nothing since morning, and the Quik satisfied us greatly.

After we had our Quik drinks, we would sometimes mix things together from under the kitchen sink—bottles and jars of cleaning fluids and noxious chemicals. Once my mother had complained about the ants outside, which had built large mounds next to our place. So my sister got us to mix things together until they steamed and smoked in the container. We were watching a lot of sci-fi shows then, and Pumpkin liked to experiment with new ideas. Actually, there was a movie called *Them* about gigantic ants taking over the world, which I think had provoked my sister into implementing some kind of preventative measures against "them" before this show might develop into reality.

We were instructed to take the contents outside, and my brother and the neighbor's kids from down the road poured it down an anthill. I didn't want to hurt the ants, so I refused. My sister watched the procedure like she watched TV, though with an intensity, a curiosity. She had beautiful dark eyes, skin, and hair blunt cut just above her shoulders; her face was round and attractive; and her skinny legs and arms stuck out from her shorts and shirt like brown pencils. Pumpkin did not participate in the ant-ridding attempt—she directed it. She was the leader among us.

Suddenly, the queens developing in the nest of the mound hatched all at once, climbing to the surface and taking flight to breed and make their own hills somewhere else. It was beautiful. The air filled with wings and hard bodies—a buzzing of red, flying ant bodies in blue above us. They then swarmed and stung and bit my brother, my sister, and the other kids, and I was the only one untouched. Afterward, I convinced myself I'd been spared because the ants knew I didn't want to kill them. Young and naive, I truly believed them my friends. We all sneakily entered the house before Mom awoke, and Pumpkin doctored my brother and herself before putting us back over the gate to pretend we were sleeping.

My childhood was forged schizophrenically by primal parental forces, grounded firmly through my father's trust, tales, and our Indian traditions while buffeted by the howling Bugger winds of my mother's insanity. What my father constructed, my mother's illness threatened to tear apart. I was easily read to sleep by the Burgess Bedtime Storybooks and comforted with traditional stories by my father. But I cried uncontrollably when learning to read by myself with the book given for such by my mother, *Beautiful Joe*, the harrowing story of a dog tortured by its owners as a puppy (I was four). When asked a question, my father would give us the Indian perspective and the scientific perspective, knowledge and viewpoint sometimes offered in five, six, or seven ways; our mother compulsively shared delusional monologues and horror stories. Every year my father planted a garden in the corner of our lot, carefully arranging rows and patterns of corn, beans, squash, pumpkins, melons, gourds encircling flowers and other plants. Screaming the nursery rhyme across the row of pumpkins my sister, Pumpkin Head, had planted—"PUT HER IN A PUMPKIN SHELL AND THERE HE KEPT HER VERY WELL!"—my mother hurled the (by now) huge orange pumpkins over a nearby tall, wooden fence, treating them as enemies of the field as if she were hurling the ominous ripened shell the Buggers sent her away to.

To escape the ongoing monologue when at home, we blasted scavenged televisions and transistor radios in every room of the house (my father told us the best advantage to being Indian was the genetic talent of adapting to anything and inventing goods from what others often overlooked or threw away). *Huckleberry Hound Dog, One Adam Twelve, Dragnet, The Adams Family, My Favorite Martian, Hitchcock, Outer Limits*, and *Twilight Zone* played hour upon hour; Motown music (pop music was too clean, too white, too fantasy) poured from radios plastered to our ears, as we hid under pillows and sang and drummed away the war my mother declared on the Buggers. We would sing for hours, learning every word to every song on the air. I couldn't stand to stay inside without music—a radio, record, something to calm or motivate me, lyrics to ponder or pull me through the day, rhythms and beats. My mother heard and perceived music differently. Mom broke all of my 45s while my last favorite little girl record was playing

> *Wait till you see my sweetie bear.*
> *He's got chocolate eyes and cinnamon hair.*
> *Lips made of sugar and a fudge éclair.*
> *Oh, how I love my sweetie bear!*
> *When Night comes around he climbs in bed and*
> *cuddles up close to grandma's head. . . . zzzzzzzkkklkk.*

Enraged, my mother destroyed them to bits while mimicking the offending lyrics in her anti-Bugger voice, a sound not unlike Betty Davis in *Whatever Happened to Baby Jane* or rake prongs on concrete or starlings swarming—the sound of madness.

The cyclone of my mother's schizophrenia repeatedly tore beyond our walls, engulfing others. Not realizing her problem, she taught piano, giving cookies and cake to her students who seemed to love her, and once tried to return to work as a physiotherapist after shock treatment. Even though certified, she was only permitted to volunteer. After dropping a patient accidentally into a whirlpool bath while the Buggers were attacking her, Mom was fired and sent home immediately. She was also pretty dangerous as a driver. Hating to scrape ice from the windshield, my mother would drive our car (at the time a Studebaker Lark) blinded in heavy storms. And more than once she would tell me, Pumpkin, and our brother, "Put YOUR SEAT belts ON! The BUGGERS are going to MAKE us wreck!" Without giving us time to buckle up, however, she would accelerate suddenly and hit or sideswipe a nearby car. I remember after one such accident calling home for her on the police radio. Not wanting to tell my dad what she'd done, I pretended to be on a television show: "One Adam Twelve. Is this Daddy?" My dad finally took away her license, claiming she'd lost it.

Dad took care of everything we couldn't. He sewed dresses for Pumpkin and me, ones like his sisters wore when they were young, only ours were made from store-bought cotton and theirs sewn from calico flour sacks. As the youngest of nine children, he had learned to do all the boys' and girls' work, so that he could take care of himself in case his parents weren't around for him. He later taught me to cook, clean, change tubes and wires on televisions and radios, change tires and brake shoes, and work on cabinets and put in Sheetrock. He said, "Someone who can't take care of himself is a burden to someone else." Every year he bought us a pair of new shoes and a new coat, the latter a coat off the spring clearance rack in a good store that was put on layaway for the next fall. Our father earned a decent federal salary, but with my mom's illness, my parents' never ending generosity to others, and their complete lack of budgeting ability, there was never enough.

But we persevered during those times of peace and stability. My dad began to bring me blues harps, and I started writing songs during my preschool years, the first with Pumpkin, named, "It's a One-Way Street," about going the wrong way. We were both always writing, always creating. My first poem was published in the school newspaper; Pumpkin and I read to each other classic literature on my mother's shelf. We enjoyed Shakespeare, Doyle, Dumas, and Edgar Allen Poe (whom I loved best of all because his worrying and obsessing struck home).

Music was our refuge in more ways than one, but not always. Once Pumpkin was selected to play with an all-city orchestra in a concert (true to our father's family heritage, we were both musically inclined, playing violins by second grade and also picking up other stringed instruments—she a mandolin and I a guitar). We had never attended a formal event: instruments being tuned, the concert hall bustling with men in tailored suits and women in fine dresses, some sporting mink or fox stoles even though it wasn't cold, it felt unreal. Wearing a white blouse and a black pleated skirt, Pumpkin performed far below our nearly ceiling-level seats. She looked so tiny, her round face, brown skin, dark hair, and thick glasses all shining under the lights. She played well, she was beautiful, and my heart felt full. I couldn't wait to tell my friends.

About midpoint during the performance, my mother declared

fresh battle with her torturers. Her voice rose high above the string section like a De Sade solo, carrying forth across our seating section. People began to motion for her to be quiet, the mostly upper-middle-class white crowd waving their hands as if flecking bugs from their shoulders and, instead of wrinkling up their noses, flaring nostrils into the air where eyes belonged and quickly turning their heads away while fanning themselves with the programs. Pumpkin was immersed in the music and so far away she never heard the outburst. Afterward my mother continued her screams and threats across the parking lot and into our white-and-red Plymouth Fury. My dad drove straight to the Underwood asylum, and (yes) men in white coats rushed out to get her.

Clutching my shirt and refusing to let go, her face twisted and contorted with turmoil and agony, my mother hollered, begged, and pleaded, "Don't let them TAKE me! They'll DESTROY my MI-nd! HELP me! HELP ME! THEY'LL RAPE ME!" She was so strong during an episode that it took several attendants, nurses, and doctors to restrain her and put her in a straitjacket. My shirt tearing from her grasp, I felt as though I was being ripped open like fish we had once gutted at Buffalo Lake.

While they restrained her, I had to restrain myself. Every bit of me wanted to fix everything somehow and take care of her and protect her. No matter how much I loved her, no matter how much I just wanted everything to stop, no matter the looming terror inside the asylum, no matter the countless days and nights I had spent praying for some release, some miracle to happen, some lifting, I had to accept a complete lack of control over the situation and disassociate. I drowned out my consciousness, my feelings of responsibility, with memories of the music my sister had played so beautifully moments ago.

Inside, where we visited her, the rooms were filled with people (mostly women) in blue and white hospital gowns slit up the back and in checked or polka-dotted pajamas. Sometimes they would brush by us and ask us for cigarettes even though we were so young. They might even touch us, bring their cold fingers to our cheeks as if to certify our realness. Sometimes we had to wait behind walls with thick glass embedded with chicken wire. Tourists. The temperature inside

Underwood and the Pavilion was typically even colder than in regular hospitals. There were high walls rimmed with windows fifteen feet up, a constant reminder of the world the residents weren't allowed to participate in. We knew Mom probably wouldn't know us. She rarely did after she came outside, so why should she inside? It was even harder for us to recognize her, I think. Her skin would pale an abnormal shade; there would always be black and purple bruising on her upper arms and under her eyes. Sometimes the bruising would yellow and swell. The electrified hair crowning my mother's weathering face looked as if it had been bristled many times since they took her away.

It was heartbreaking, and I prayed hard every morning and each night for the Buggers to leave her alone.

My prayers were never answered. Despite our compassion, despite our singing, despite our various clever attempts at avoidance and escape, and despite the best efforts of my father, we suffered. Our childhood companion and enemy, the Buggers, constantly denigrated and punished us, their maniacal torrent of voices and actions through my mother threatening to fracture the foundation of self-worth, identity, and family ties being built from the stones of my father's stories and our combined heritage.

We dreaded the times for the family to gather—holiday seasons—because our mother expected us to be sick with dreaded diseases: measles, mumps, rubella, chicken pox, you name it. As the era dictated, trying to protect us from them, she intentionally exposed us to the diseases by taking us to infected children's homes ten days before the holiday and making us play with them (even if they were really sick and throwing up) until she felt we were contaminated. In a week or two, we too would break out with rashes or quiver with chills. Pumpkin, usually very healthy, would become really sick. I fought off most of the communicable diseases and fooled everyone the rest of the time by pretending to be well. Thermometer by a cold window, hot baths to flush out a rash—I did not want to stay home, sick or not. We learned to hate the holidays. They were like punishment. We were thrilled when they came up with new vaccinations to prevent sicknesses, but we truly hated shots as well.

Intentional punishments from my mother were inconsistent.

Once—before I have clear memory—while living in a rural area, Pumpkin and I were carrying in our overhauls chicken eggs we'd gathered for Mom. Somehow we dropped one of the eggs and Mom spanked us, smashing the pocketfuls of eggs we'd gathered and flooding our pants with egg slime. Infuriated by the mistake, my mother forced us to sit on a black rubber tire in the hot northern Texas Panhandle sun until our father came home and found us, sunbaked, with eggs cooked into our dungarees.

My sister and I were punished with hands and convenient implements. Pumpkin sometimes panicked and tried to protect herself. Once when she put her arm behind her bottom to stop our mother from making contact with a fly swatter, its wire broke and went inside the skin up her wrist. If we were injured during a punishment or by accident, we were supposed to sit on the concrete slab outside the front door and wait for Dad to come home from work—no matter what time of day we got hurt. During that long day, I sat with Pumpkin, the fly swatter hanging out of her hand like a piercing rod, waiting for my Dad to come home and take her to the doctor. He looked so sad to see her hurt like that, his face dropping its expression entirely. We felt terrible too, wanting him to think everything was fine every day when he came home.

On another occasion, Pumpkin was intimidated into learning how to ride a bike. She had gotten a newer used bike—blue, big, and with a bell on the right-hand grip. She had had a hard time learning to peddle and hold the bike up, but one day my mother became suddenly determined that she would learn. She chased Pumpkin around a vacant lot next to our place, dress billowing in the wind, screaming at the Buggers and threatening to hit my sister with the fly swatter in her right hand or the belt in her left if she fell. My little red bike came from B and D's trading post and still had training wheels. Riding in circles around them during the bike lesson, as if in orbit around two polarized masses of energy, silver spokes clicking past dried grasses and dust like huge vaccination needles.

The most consistent and vehement target of my mother's outbursts, however, was me. She reminded me many times that I was the "extra girl" and the most deserving of Bugger punishment. My sister was the oldest and was spared some of the "girl punishment" because she was the first of my mother's children to survive. My younger brother was her favorite child—Mom believed our brother could do no wrong, and everything he did to get her attention went as excusable behavior since the Buggers "MADE him do it." She claimed they had had me when they were trying for him, so I, as the "extra girl," had to take care of my brother; that her mother had favored male children to female; and that girls needed more "punishment."

I was the "bad" girl, always needing the most severe discipline, fixing, and changing: I was wrong somehow. I was disciplined for wearing blue clothes on numerous occasions, usually just before leaving for school; it was my favorite color, but she loathed blue because it denoted governmental authorities like the police. My mother used to tell me she'd hated me since the day I was born. I am unsure why I was selected, maybe because I was the second girl or the lightest—the "Indian blonde," the "dirty blonde," the only "blondie"—hair labels I carried despite the fact that my hair was actually a light golden brown (hair labels my dad tried to alleviate by first telling me all the dumb blondes in Hollywood were actually brunettes who bleached their hair with peroxide and then recalling many lighter-haired women who were known for bravery, courage, and great intelligence). Her lack of belief in my value as a daughter was evident when talking about the future. Pumpkin could be a bad girl "at times," but she was normally the "smart" girl and would "go far in life." Pumpkin would be the greatest writer in the world, the greatest leader—she was told she could do whatever she wanted to do—and my brother was taught that whatever he did he would be a "great man." In contrast, we were all told that *if* I was *lucky* I might find someone who had a business who would *let* me keep their books for them or something. Also, when my mother was home with us, she would assign to me additional tasks that emphasized my responsibility to keep things in order. She would curse the Buggers while I scrubbed enamel-painted baseboards or the toilet (not my favorite thing to clean, but doing so prevented her from accidentally using our face cloths instead of a cloth rag to wipe it off). She frequently gave away my toys or destroyed them.

My mother's differential treatment and divide-and-conquer tactics with her children, strictly a result of the schizophrenia, took their toll on how we felt about ourselves and toward each other. Pumpkin and I, who had always been close, began to grow distant from all the tension at home. Once I came home from second grade and went into our room. There were piles of fake fur scraps everywhere. The animals' eyes were hanging out like they'd been hit by trains, the hides slit clean off the bellies and strewn everywhere. It looked like a butchering for a big feed, only as if someone had to butcher all the pets in a pinch to provide meat. Sitting on the floor in the midst of the stuffing and looking over at Pumpkin's bed, I saw her dolls were all wearing fur coats and lying in fur sleeping bundles freshly sewn together. I leapt to ask her why she took my toys apart, and, smiling, she told me our mother told her to do it. That night I slept next to my dad's dog, Ginger, and two of our other dogs on the tile floor. I remember them breathing and running in their sleep.

When John F. Kennedy was killed, my sister came home early from school because of the shooting. My mother was lambasting the Buggers, speaking directly to the stove ventilation bugging device, condemning the federal government for plots, schemes, assassinations, and conspiracies long before my sister arrived. When Pumpkin suddenly slammed the screen door, Mom had already left the kitchen and was playing her old upright Steinway in the living room. When she told her the president had been murdered, my mother said, "Oh, you kids will say anything. Ha, Ha, Ha, Ha! Eh." And she played some "Finlandia," laughing to herself. Pumpkin's cat-eye glasses almost camouflaged a strange stare in her brown eyes, but I noticed and imagined Kennedy as a presidential ghost while watching TV reporters play the Dallas tapes over and over. I wondered why my mother didn't take this assassination personally since she constantly lectured the evils of the American government and blamed them for everything wrong without exception before this time.

When Pumpkin was very angry with me, especially if I didn't do things the way she expected me to, she would claim that the reason I was so light was because I was adopted (and I would sometimes look in the mirror and begin to believe it). Despite our continual taunts and fights at home, I always stood up for her against outsiders at school.

My brother pulled a long string of pranks to get my mother's attention—setting fire to new houses, shooting birds without intending to eat them, dirtying a room after I had cleaned it, breaking windows, or using me as a target for his BB pellet gun or knife-throwing games. Mom would not allow anyone to discipline him and would strike my dad if he tried to punish my brother in any way. Knowing I was not allowed to hit back, my brother began beating me up as soon as he outgrew me. Pumpkin was bigger than both of us, and they would clash quite often. I'd sometimes run for an adult neighbor to come stop them.

Our fights were serious—bones broken, flesh chewed out, walls and windows smashed. Once Pumpkin and our brother locked me out of the kitchen and into the garage. Having watched jousting knights in television movies, I tried similarly to ram the door down with a broom handle. The door did not budge, but, being cheap and hollow, it was easily penetrated by the broom handle, leaving a perfect circle the size of a fifty-cent piece. Pumpkin opened the door and the fight ended. When my dad came home he looked directly at us but never said a word, quietly repairing the door like he had rebuilt and replaced walls and windows before. Pumpkin and I felt terrible and barely left our room that night.

Strong and resourceful as I was on the outside, my mother's craziness and harassment, as well as the fights with my brother and sister, affected me deeply. I was late to school frequently in first grade because my mother found additional tasks for me to complete before I could leave in the morning—picking up dog feces near the porch, scrubbing the enamel-painted baseboards with a toothbrush. Walking into class late, I was in trouble immediately, my teacher demanding an explanation of my whereabouts and I saying nothing to avoid talking back or revealing my mother's illness. Announcing that I was lazy and belligerent, my teacher would send me to the principal's office each time. As punishment for my tardiness and bad attitude, the principal would hit me with a wooden board punctuated with drilled holes, blistering my skin where it landed.

No matter how hard or how many times the principal struck, I did not shed tears or complain. Knowing fully well he would only hit me harder if I did not cry, I nonetheless took the swats, did not tell family secrets, and did not look into the principal's face. I was steadfast. I did not tell anyone what was going on, not even my father, because I was ashamed of being a lazy, belligerent, bad girl. I continued to do my housework and other chores when my mother asked, continued to be late, and learned to put up with rough treatment as a part of school life. I would not cry again for years.

So, as we ducked under elementary school desks during atomic bomb drills in the 1960s, read increasingly about current Vietnam events in the same *Weekly Reader* that introduced Rookie of the Year Joe Namath and featured a tribe in Africa who allegedly had only two toes and used them to climb trees, I learned an essential lesson: no one would ever make me cry again. During a time when we were taught that our paths were many and myriad careers possible—boxer, bronc rider, jockey, firefighter, forest ranger, heavy equipment or bus driver—I came to realize that the greatest tangible control I could gain over my life was to shut down the part of me they wanted to punish and to protect it the only way I knew how. I wanted to be unnoticed.

There was always so much going on in our house (because of my mom's illness and my dad's hours on his federal job) that it was easy for things to go unnoticed. I began suffering tonsillitis in first grade along with chronic ear infections. The clinic doctors would lance my eardrums with long metal needles, then check my throat and prescribe antibiotics. The antibiotic shots hurt much more than any other shot I'd had, except for local anesthetics. When my teeth were worked on, I couldn't tolerate the numbing shots, so my dad taught me to sing in my mind and ignore the physical pain so the teeth could be drilled with nothing. It helped if the dentist wore glasses, because you could watch the procedure in the reflection on the lenses and ignore the pain with the focused distraction. Antibiotics hurt too, and I would bite leather my dad brought with him to the doctor or bite his finger, until I once bit it so hard he decided not to offer it again.

First grade was a yearlong bout with tonsillitis and ear infections. I'd faked well and gone to school as much as I could, but much days were lost nonetheless. Once during this year, my mother's parents decided nothing was wrong with "their daughter" and that my dad must be doing something wrong to cause all of her "so-called problems." They sort of kidnapped all of us from him, including my mother. My dad took an extra assignment at work and waited it out. We didn't fully realize we were being taken from him because my mother was along and we spent all our summers and quite a lot of time in Canada anyway.

On the trip north, we hit an area in Montana where wondering if your last gas fill-up would make the next town was not for lack of stopping at the last station. There were no stations between these towns in those days.

I was sweating. And because we were locked in the car all together, it was impossible to conceal. My mother was telling her parents about the Buggers, and our grandmother was telling Mom my father must be making all of "this" happen. "Hazel, our doctor said that nothing was wrong with you," she had written her in letters to the institution, claiming she would be fine as soon as she returned to Canada. We knew what "this" was. It was the war with the Buggers. We also knew my dad was never in on the war at all. This grandmother was not like us. She was not mixed-racial. Just mixed-European. To her we were all "siewashes" and beneath her somehow. Her own blood relatives. Descendants. Offspring. We also knew this grandfather would never stand up to her. He might not join in, but he would never go against her. The chance of repercussion was far too great.

Grandma wanted to take Mom to a hospital in Lethbridge. We didn't make it that far. All three of us kids came down simultaneously with tonsillitis, and the fevers put us in the first hospital we passed with an emergency room. I was kicking and fighting all the way in. It was a Catholic hospital, known to treat for free in emergency situations. Penicillin was coming. I'd had it before. The shot would burn my leg and half paralyze me for the day, and no one would believe it hurt like it did. Then the "pink angels" came, assistants to the nurses and doctors and I think maybe volunteering Catholics in the hospital or Catholic Candy Stripers. It took several pink angels, some nurses, nuns, and a doctor to give me the shot. One of the nuns got kicked square in the face on the way down. Going down fighting was the only way for Hedgecokes to go down.

We eventually made it to Lethbridge. I suppose they confirmed my mom's madness because soon we all ended up on my grandparents' place west of Spring Coulee. They had a great place—deer, moose, horses, cattle, crab apples, strawberries (my favorite food besides wild rose petals, so good fresh picked you could not keep Pumpkin and me away from them), a red pitcher pump that brought sweet water with each draw—all surrounded by the Rockies, ice-melt lakes, and cottonwood trees. It was beautiful. We loved their home even though we felt unwelcome. We usually just enjoyed our surroundings and stayed clear of our grandmother altogether. My grandfather was nice to us, had us in the saddle with him before we could walk, rode us out to check his livestock, and took us with him to hay, but because his wife was so hard I, Baby No, used to tell him my dad could beat him up and that we had twice as many horses as he did (of course, I was counting all the horses in the community as ours).

My mother's parents got what they wanted. But soon Grandma was so fed up with all of us she started wondering if they should have brought us at all. In a few weeks they took us all back down to my dad and let us out in the driveway. They couldn't handle my mother any better than we could, and Grandma didn't have much compassion for us either. My dad wasn't surprised in the least and only said, "What took you so long?"

I hate to think about it, but many times I begged my dad to leave my mom. I'd beg and ask if we could stay permanently in Oklahoma (where we imagined we would fit in) with Auntie Rose, leaving Mom in the care of her own parents. He was always patient in answering, explaining that it was his duty to stay with her—she was his wife, our mother, and no matter what happened we couldn't leave her. She was sick and couldn't help it, and I needed to be strong. He claimed she would get better some day, and when that occurred we would see her the same way he still did—younger, happy, healthy, and in love with him. My father never left my mother all those long, crazy years.

In second grade the tonsils had to go. My parents waited from August until February, because they were so "busy" that year. Every once in a while, Pumpkin would come tell me it was time for my surgery, then laugh, "Aaayee," to tease me. During a winter storm, my class was watching a *Loony Toons* film in the "cafetorium" at school. The shades were drawn, and it was quiet except for the cartoon. Pumpkin came and whispered for me to follow her, saying that it was time to go.

My dad took me to the hospital and for some reason was still sitting in my room after they had completely checked me in. When I asked him why, he told me that he thought I might like some company, that it was a sort of major operation, to which I replied that I was a big girl and needn't be sat with all night just for a major operation. So he stood and shook my hand and told me I was his bravest kid and left for the night.

In the hospital I couldn't sleep well because of the voices from other kids and the crying, but also because I kept seeing faces around me in the room and I wasn't sure who they were. I did fall asleep deeply enough when they placed something damp over my face and told me to count backward from ten.

After the surgery, I was surprised I couldn't see well, or swallow, or breathe, or think, or talk normally at all. I whispered that I'd like very much to see what they'd removed. "No, no, no," the doctor told me, "no," because my tonsils were green. Green. I thought whatever was cut from you was red like meat. I'd never seen green meat in an animal; the idea seemed unreal. He whispered, as if he had had his own throat cut, that the tonsils had gangrene in them and had almost killed me. He said I should have had them out much sooner . . . "much sooner."

Hardening, I strove incessantly to excel, never giving up in the classroom or in track, baseball, basketball, or P.E. class. Gathering ribbons, trophies, medals, and presidential fitness awards every year of grade school, beating the best, running the farthest, and hanging on the longest were goals. I cared more about surpassing my own accomplishments, however, than about competing with others. Once in fourth grade, while attempting a flexed-arm hang in P.E. class, I held on so long that the lunch bell rang, the class left, but I couldn't let go until I set a record. All that existed was the timer and me, hanging on a bar above the floor, my hands crawdad claws, my body shaking violently from hanging so long, my neck muscles tensed and ready to snap. In track I always ran key or anchor for relays and beat some local school records, pushing myself so hard I often threw up. The last stretch was the most important; if anybody was close, I would pull out like a horse in a race. Having ridden horses since before I could walk, including riding some rodeo, it was easy to imagine my legs were horse legs, racing, barely touching the ground, raising high to get the distance in, stepping long, almost entirely on my toes.

Hardening, I also began fighting all the time at school, hanging tough and defending anyone who needed help, including Pumpkin. She was picked on for being dark, for her round pie face and glasses. Though there were plenty of blond girls in that particular school (though none of the blondes but me was mixed-blood), I was teased and harassed because my cheekbones and nose were two years ahead of the rest of my face—"dirty blonde" and "dirty half-breed" were slurs that I responded to with a mean upper cut and jab rather than words. During these fights, I would sometimes imagine myself as a great mountain lion without fear of any enemy; other times I became a deer thrashing hard hooves from a hind-legged stance.

My grades were good and I was an accomplished athlete, so the teachers could not understand why I got into trouble so frequently. In my insanity-goaded, mixed-blood mind there were two categories of peers: friends and enemies. Without a formal declaration of alliance, a person was suspect, but unconditional support was given to those with whom I had acknowledged friendship. I battled for and defended what should be righteous in the world. The only person I didn't fight at least once was Linda Hammond, my first best friend. Linda's mom was Indian and her dad was white, but looking at her pure Indian looks you would never know she was mixed. Linda was the kindest and most graceful girl any of us knew, never giving offense.

I was full of guts and ready to scrap out on a simple wrong look. One boy had a crush on me, making him instantly suspect; though I punched him out daily on the way to school, each morning he would be standing there, waiting for more. If kids were ganging up on someone and it wasn't a fair fight (whether I knew the victim or not) I'd dive in and take a few down. I even fought a preacher's daughter who lived down the road—well, it wasn't much of a fight. White and about my same age but bigger, she often stood outside her house and taunted us. I ignored her until the day she called Pumpkin and me "pagan heathens" one too many times. I had no idea what the racial slur meant, but her tone of voice could not be tolerated. Walking over, I went for her nose right away, breaking it in one shot, a straight uppercut. After the preacher called my father that evening, rather than getting angry with me for defending us, Dad looked like he was holding back a smile. Trying his best to frown, he did admit that my actions had probably proven the preacher's daughter correct. After that day, though, she never stood outside her house when we walked passed, never taunted us again. I also refused to take insults on the softball field. I was fast, a good fielder and crack hitter (especially if jeered at by pitchers for being short and skinny), but I wasn't allowed to pitch because my fastball might purposely knock out the batters if they made me mad.

Sometime in second or third grade I became self-destructive, hurting myself before Mom could punish me. I attempted suicide a few times, feeling responsible for our family problems and shame and believing if I were out of the way things might get better for everyone else. Besides, we had been raised by my father to view death as a natural part of life, a change of worlds, and thus nothing to fear. Life was hard here and seemed better over there. I remember once my mother screaming at me and locking myself in the bathroom, where I slit my wrists with a blade from my dad's razor. I didn't make the cuts right, however, and was forced to wrap bandannas around my wrists to conceal the naive attempt. I tried cinching a belt around my neck, but it only cut off the circulation, causing me to flop around on the floor a few times before passing out. An attempt a week later to hang myself failed because the rope broke when I jumped off a stool in the attic.

I never told anyone about my suicide attempts. During my years in elementary school, it seemed at times that no one noticed much of what I did—I even stopped eating for stretches to see if my family would notice. I was frail and often sickly, though I hated to be ill. There was so much tumult and chaos in our house all the time that it was easy for problems to go unnoticed. Something must have made at least my father aware of my difficulties, however, because he began taking me on long walks out in the country and continued telling me about living and Indian beliefs in the Great Spirit and the Spirit World (my mom approved but also decided Pumpkin and I should sing for God in an Episcopal choir in Latin). I began to see around me what I believed to be ghosts more regularly about this time. Whether singing with my dad or in a choir, I would see faces and sometimes hear whispers of my name from nowhere. These couldn't be the same voices my mother heard because they were good, calming, and gave me peace. Maybe just my imagination, I thought, like the boats I saw when I was smaller.

Prayers and death became familiar and complementary companions during those elementary school years of silent endurance and flashes of anger. I began to invite kids over to pray with me in our toolshed. I offered to bury their dead dogs and cats, or strays run over on the road, or birds that our brothers had killed. If a couple of girls came to pray even once I felt that our prayers must be stronger and someone would surely come help us soon. Praying and burying kept me from harming myself much. Dad approved—burial was a good thing, producing fertilizer for our corn in the years to come. Curious about decay, I sometimes dug up and reburied things to see the process at work.

I began to drink and smoke, tasting alcohol first at the age of eight. Whiskey was added to a girlfriend's and my sodas by her father (who called it a "special float"). He prepared the drink like Pumpkin and I used to mix chemicals and cleaners stored below our kitchen sink, and it smelled like fumes from siphoning gasoline. My girlfriend smiled and drank, and so did I. Many times we rode with her father to the bootleggers or to bars and liquor stores, where he would leave us in the car with Penrose sausages or potato chips. On the way home, drinking and driving, he'd point out places where drunk-driving relatives had been killed. We could almost see it all happening, collision and death under train trestles or off embankments.

The potentially deadly effects of alcohol were made even clearer to me the time some older boys from my friend Becky Goodnight's neighborhood gave my friends and me some wine. Cheryl, a half-Tejana girl, had a reaction to it and went into a coma. Frightened, I crept back into our house through a window with a girlfriend, we dove under the covers, and the cops arrived. My father's insistence that we were home all along—punctuated by my mother railing against the political crimes of the police department—was rendered moot when the police pulled the covers down and saw we were fully clothed, complete with dusty shoes. We were taken in for questioning. The girl survived, but the experience taught me about intolerance to alcohol. It didn't stop me from drinking, but I wasn't innocent about its power anymore.

I learned some vices from my parents. They were both chain smokers; Dad loved tobacco, and Mom smoked because he did. Pumpkin and I would steal their smokes when they weren't looking. My parents also loved coffee—thick, black, and boiled—which we also really liked, drinking coffee with them from the time we could first sit at the table. Although the caffeine made us shake, it seemed natural since my father shook all the time from an essential familial tremor (consequently, oftentimes I was his hands when he was refinishing a piece of furniture, working on a television or radio, or fixing up a cabinet).

By the age of nine, my family situation was increasingly difficult to conceal. Stories about my insane parent and gossip about my family were circulating behind my back among classmates, making it hard to trust peers and to invite anyone over. I felt taboo, out of place at home and in school, and I just wanted it to stop. I could play ball, run track, ride horses, and do math, but I did not know how—or have the heart to learn how—to gossip and play manipulative games like my classmates did. Such complex and devious ways of socialization and purposes of behaviors were difficult to fathom, harder to practice. The main social lesson I learned had been to accept undeserved punishment and to turn away or leave. And so I did. I quit hanging around with most of the kids my age and looked for some new friends, seeking a place where people could not twist the truth.

And so began a search and a wandering, a string of leavings, that have continued through the years.

I added another "l" to my middle name for alliteration and control of my own identity. I moved in with my baseball coach, Donna, when I was nine years old. Nearly eighteen, she lived with her mom and a sister (who was my age), their dad having accidentally blown his brains out over the living room walls while deciding whether or not to shoot his wife. They treated me well. I drank, smoked, and hung out with Donna and one of her friends, Rita, riding around in Donna's car all summer and stopping at places visiting mostly teenagers.

My family made no fuss or argument over my leaving; I was able to take care of my physical needs, could cook and clean and do what was needed to get by, and was expected to make my own decisions and stick by them. After deciding to leave home, I called my father, asking for a brown suitcase I'd prepacked with shorts, jeans, T-shirts, and underwear. Bringing it to me, he shook my hand and simply said, "Write when you get work, kid," a phrase I would hear many times in the years after. My father, I learned much later, dealt with this change as he had others in his life—through trust, tolerance, and quiet guidance. He knew that, if he had opposed the departure of the "extra girl," Baby No might never have returned.

When I was about ten, the Buggers plagued one of our annual trips to visit relatives. While taking my mother to visit her parents in Canada, we had intended to attend the Crow Fair in Montana but missed the event due to car trouble and bad weather. Although disappointed, we managed still to stop at the Little Bighorn battlefield, which my dad called Greasy Grass. Each time we went there, he would describe the battle with detail, excitement, and great satisfaction, drawing in the dirt how it had been fought and reminding us about the objects my Huron/French-Canadian grandma had received from a Cheyenne Dog Soldier who had been part of the battle at the Little Bighorn and had claimed her years later as a daughter when she was still a young girl (who by then had relocated to Indian Territory). Even though my family was descended from other tribes, we were most impressed with the victory won at that place.

After we had ordered hamburgers in a Hardin café the next day, some young Indian men came over to talk to my dad, asking where he was from and about his tribe—all of the regular questions of greeting—and introducing him to older people there. My father returned, ate with us, and then announced that he wanted to stay and dance with these men in a ceremonial. When the young Indian men came over again to chat, my mother—who had been especially lucid the whole trip—erupted in a tirade against the Buggers in front of the entire café, now adding dancing to the regular complaints and accusing my dad of wanting to leave her there though we were already late on our trip to Canada. My dad quickly paid the cashier, shook hands all around, calmly said, "Maybe another time," and escorted us out as pleasantly as he could amid her screaming.

When we got to the car, Dad put Mom, Pumpkin, and my brother in the back seat and then told me, "If you can talk her into being quiet I'll give you a dollar."

All right! I thought, *I can do this.*

I asked Mom, "Why do you yell at the Buggers all the time?"

"Because they are torturing me," she replied. "They *make* me yell at them!"

I then suggested, "Why don't you make them mad? Why don't you be really quiet and then they can't get what they want?"

"Huhn," she said, quieting down, her face still contorted and her muscles wracked by spasms, until she fell asleep. After crossing the border, my dad stopped at Cardston and paid me my dollar without anyone else knowing.

Of course, these fleeting moments of peace would not last, and she would return to the asylum again and again.

When we visited her in the Pavilion that fall, a nurse gave us a Tonto and Lone Ranger toy set to busy ourselves so my dad could try to visit with my mom. I felt we were too old for the toys; though my brother was only slightly younger than I was, it seemed like he was just a little guy, and he was very impressionable. He took the Lone Ranger and started shooting at Tonto. I laughed at his frenzy war with the plastic figures and finally shot an arrow for Tonto right into Lone Ranger's forehead (or at least that's what I imagined). My brother (in the white masked man role), having watched too much tv, said, "I'm going to get you, you dirty Indian."

Instantaneously, from the thick haze she seemed consumed in, my mother's hearing was suddenly acute. She jumped toward us screaming, "DON'T YOU EVER TALK LIKE THAT!"

"Hazel," my dad said, "he's only copying the television. He knows he's Indian. He's just playing," putting his hand gently on her shoulder to console her. We left very saddened, knowing that her outburst would yield another shock treatment.

On the way home the radio played this hit song: "They're coming to take you away. Ha, ha, he, he, ho, ho. To the funny farm . . ."

Who could possibly deny that the firewater the
colonists used in early chemical warfare on
Western Hemisphere peoples was, of course, a
far slower method of destruction, but one soon
test proven just as deadly as the germ warfare–
induced smallpoxed trade blankets. Who can
deny that while smallpox proved immediately
fatal, alcohol cripples in ways even multiple gen-
erations cannot sort through. With the peoples
thus effectively diminished and handicapped,
the dominating oppressor successfully separated
children from their caretaker relatives and
educated them with colonial ideals, hoping to
finish off the leftovers from the spoils. Many
families still keep braids their ancestors had cut
forcibly from their heads upon entering school.
For generations now, the education system has
employed a generous multitude of tactics to con-
trol, to civilize, and to educate children. These
exceptionally effective methods of genocide were
utilized with purposeful intent and great malice.

3

When Fire and Water Meet

One summer night my father woke us from hard sleep and persuaded Pumpkin, my brother, and me to follow him out back. Shooting and falling stars blazed burning, fleeting paths across the entire Southern Plains sky, so many that you could barely imagine the sky so full. Our upturned heads were greeted by sheer brilliance and fiery displays of light, chaos demonstrating perfect rhythm and patterned order.

On this wondrous night and others, we would stargaze and Dad would explain how important cosmology was to our people, telling of mounds and lodgings in our homelands back east, of an image of a woman riding a horse on the moon's face, of our people's migrations and the significance of motion, of long-ago paintings created precisely below certain stellar movements and positions, and of how all things were planted by the timing of certain moons and solstices. We learned that there was a time and place for everything in our universe, that we were grains in a perpetual orbiting mass. Places have memory; when we travel, we would be recognized in North Carolina and in Canada, where our ancestors lay, and in the stars above. Our father taught us this, and we were infatuated.

Our dad also spoke to us about such topics as science and chemistry. Early on he had taught me square roots and basic algebraic equations—while studying refresher courses for his job, he kept me from bothering him (too much) by writing some problems on paper, explaining what to do, and having me solve them. We used numbers to play binary code puzzles and other games and were well aware that when leaves fell they were filled with anthocyanin. The periodic table was not an uncommon chart in our home.

I became truly interested in math and science, hoping at one point to follow in my father's footsteps, and I also became increasingly interested in creative pursuits like music, writing, poetry, and painting. By sixth grade, however, the never ending ordeal of home, the toughness I had cultivated to deal with it, and my inherent intelligence made my schooling more of a challenge and a problem than it needed to be. I was often bored in classes, and, due to sleep lost to my mother's nightly hysteria, I would be exhausted after half a day, sleeping or daydreaming through the afternoon classes. Sometimes I'd sit around wondering how things would be different if Indian people had won the war for the Western Hemisphere or if the moon really looked like it did on television when Neil A. Armstrong first touched the gray ground above.

My sixth grade math and science teacher, Mr. Austin—whose class was late in the day, unfortunately—had no patience for me. I pulled good grades in both subjects in his classroom, but he treated me like a slacker. He'd toss a pop quiz on my desk while I was catching up on sleep, banging hard with a ruler to wake me to the test. Because I usually aced the exam in minutes and would resume napping, Mr. Austin's punishment for sleeping worsened—almost daily I was forced to stand on one leg in a corner, my nose in contact with a chalked circle on the blackboard, my neck sore because the circle was intentionally drawn a few inches higher than my nose. Directly above the circle hung a board with the words "Allison's Corner" burned into the wood.

Mr. Austin's persecution finally ended, ironically, because of my mother's actions. Delusional, chasing me for dropping butter on the floor, my mother had grabbed fly swatters to hit me with and then the phone, which came down on the back of my neck. Since she didn't realize she had made contact and kept swinging, I turned, wrenched the phone from her, and hit myself with it, yelling, "Here, I'll do it for you!"

"Am-er-i-can Me-di-cal As-so-ci-a-tion! AN-gli-can CHURCH! P-T-A! PO-lice De-part-ment! POLICE! Quit RAP-ing-me with your RA-di-o WAVES! Stay OFF my vul-va! You DAMN DIR-ty pimps! QUIT RAPING ME!"

Later that night, dozens of lymph nodes, round, hard, and flat, had swelled across the back of my neck. Pumpkin suggested showing them to Mr. Austin so he would assume I was sick and leave me alone. The next day I walked up to him quietly and said I couldn't stand in the corner because I needed to sit down and rest. He took me out in the hall and demanded to know why I was openly disrespecting him. Lifting up my hair—as Pumpkin had advised me—I showed him my neck. His face changing expression, Mr. Austin muttered, "Just get back to your seat." I never had to stand in the corner again, and, in fact, he barely spoke to me for the rest of the year.

The art teacher that year didn't perceive me as a model student either. My father's stories about Indian paintings marking trails and the rise and fall of the sun had inspired me to perceive color as something to brush chaos with. I decided to paint the bedroom myself, applying a rich pink, textured paint (intended for ceilings) that, to me, looked like huge rose petals lined with thousands of dew globules. The painted walls would spike you if you leaned against them, but they survived a tornado that took out the west side of our house and some roof. My art teacher was less appreciative of my sensibility and effort. In class we were drawing with oil pastels, and I was layering the colors thicker and thicker, almost breaking the fancy crayons to get the thickness right, wanting the bright colors waxy, thick as tar. As she darted across the room to stop me from wasting colors, my bubble gum popped; the teacher sat me on a stool in front of the room, put the gum on my nose, and left me there for the remainder of the class. Eventually my hair fell on my nose, and the gum got stuck in it. When the students started laughing, she took a large pair of metal shears and sliced away the hair hanging in front of my face connected to the gum. After school the art teacher reprimanded me for layering the colors—"why can't you just use pastels lightly like all the other kids? And why do you dig your nails into the paints? Do you think we finger-paint here?"

My mother also whacked off my hair without shape or pattern. She called this getting a "hairdo." Hair would fall in hunks of varying length from different places off my head, and I would wonder while she was cutting who would fix it. Sometimes a white woman named Billie, up the road from us, would take me into her backyard and give me a "trim." Several times Mom tried to perm my straight hair, placing a curler here and there in no particular order, so that for the next few weeks my hair would be straight-curl-up, up-straight-curl, down-straight-curl-curl. I looked like a curler experiment, and no one could shape up the "perm." I had to wait until it grew out.

When we were smaller, my dad would take us along to the barbershop with him, to spare us Mom's "dos." By now we were so obviously girls we couldn't get away with boys' cuts because of the price difference. So the kids at school were already familiar with my hair suddenly being chopped away in bits and pieces, already familiar with me walking in fresh cut with my fists tight and ready. Sitting in front of the class and having it cut sliced away the veil of mystery, my identity secret until now. My spirit split from my crown and wandered off. I wanted to become invisible. I was ghosting. I soon found being invisible was perilous, as well.

In contrast to other faculty, Mrs. Minor, my English teacher, who had enjoyed my sister as a student, accepted my differences but never really understood them, encouraging yet ultimately naive. She nudged me to write stories and poems for extra credit. Inspired by the title for the movie *Diary of a Mad Housewife* (I was too young to see the film and had never read the book), I decided to write a novel called *Diary of a Mad Housewife's Daughter*. Working diligently in my dad's toolshed, I carefully compiled the book from my journal notes.

Toward the end of the school year, I left the manuscript, wrapped in a paper sack, with Mrs. Minor just before the weekend. After class the following week, she praised me on the most interesting *fiction* I had written. She didn't comprehend that the stories were real, that their author was living the diary journal. Mrs. Minor didn't see the differences that other teachers locked on to with full horns. Her face serious but serene—resembling my mother's slightly, without the tension and torment—she added that an eleven-year-old was unusually talented to write such stories and that she wanted me to meet some high school and college teacher friends of hers who were involved in writing.

A stinger lodged deep in my spine and I panicked—my English teacher intended to share this book with other adults. People who didn't already know my mother would find out about her mental illness. Grabbing the pages, I ran from the classroom and raced home, sprinting down the dirt path behind our place and jumping the short white plank fence out at the very back. Standing there was an ancient, black, cast-iron coal stove that had belonged to my dad's mother, the same stove she'd heated their dugout with and cooked food on in the early 1900s, the same one we cooked hot dogs and hamburgers on still. I pulled aside the circular metal plates on the stovetop, stuffed the manuscript down inside the belly, and set the book afire with stick matches.

Pages curled toward my face, paper blackening around the words, flames taking hold of the stories, of my mother's illness and the Buggers, of how the past winter I'd run from the house in my bare feet to escape my mother's delusions and caught pneumonia in the snow and wind, of my mother jamming Mentholatum up my nose and packing it so I couldn't breathe, of the fly swatter hits on our tender skin, and of the shock treatments and cries of governmental computer puppetry, the story of all our stories.

I carried the ashes to the garden, hoping something could grow of it.

Staying outside almost all night, I prayed my teacher wouldn't tell anyone my story. I never mourned this book, but sometimes I wonder about the lost contents: hazardous, unaffordable.

Around the time I began seventh grade, my family was being swept up by intensifying eddies of change. My schooling was generally more supportive that year — the English teacher was an eloquent Black woman who taught us things I'm sure no other faculty around us would have, giving us glimpses of Zora Neale Hurston's writings and encouraging us to deconstruct literature as an approach to its secrets. The history teacher, Mr. Klingsick, a man's man among the faculty, made bets with me on the Cassius Clay and Joe Frazier fights.

But picture me at age twelve — forty-nine pounds, dark-brown skin from the long summer, straight sun-bleached hair, gangly legs — I was awkward. To make matters worse, my adult facial features had already developed, so I had huge cheekbones and a tremendously bridged nose on a little girl's face. An obvious breed-child. And I had developed breasts. My father did not wish us to wear bras because they "interfere with the development of important muscles — the pectorals," adding that "a while back Indian women never wore bras, and they were the healthier for it and for working." Pumpkin and I some-times wore formless bras or undershirts beneath our shifts instead. By the end of the year, the boys in eighth grade were asking me to go steady instead of pushing me into sheet-metal locker doors. I began wearing a jacket all the time at school so they would forget my breasts and everyone would just leave me alone.

The web of kinship and responsibility connecting us to our rela-tives was also stretching, being rewoven, or even snapping here and there. My mother's parents sold their Alberta wheat and cattle land and moved into Lethbridge. Well past working age, they needed to be closer to hospitals because of my grandmother's angina pectoris and my grandfather's carditis. That year it was our grandparents' fiftieth wedding anniversary, and we, with all of our cousins, gathered there for the event. Pumpkin and I slept in a room down in the basement of their new place. I remember the light blue of the bed covers, so soft we were sure they were of fine quality. We missed our grand-parents' place in the country, the place our mom had grown up, the character of the house and lands surrounding it. My grandmother's harness loom now stood in the corner of the basement. The house contained familiar pieces of her work all through it, intricate weav-ings the most alive part of her, the closest thing to her soul. Her art-work was gorgeous too; mountains and streams attached themselves to paper at her whim. Pumpkin and I stayed up late one night, whis-pering together, gossiping about our relatives, and wondering why our mother's mother remained so bitter toward us. She constantly compared us unfavorably with our maternal cousins from Calgary or El Paso, constantly harping on our lack of etiquette, allowing other cousins to travel with her and Grandpa while refusing to pick up Pumpkin from a local station so that she could attend a children's council nearby. She never wanted to be seen with us even when we were staying with her. We loved her, but we desperately needed ac-ceptance.

Early one morning, my mother came downstairs carrying on a passionate monologue toward her "TOR-tur-ers." Pumpkin and I (worn out from having slept under the bed because I had lost my front tooth in my cousin's head playing rough and our uncle Ray had been drinking and was taking it out on my cousin) didn't want the relatives to hear her to further compound our problems with them. Pleading with Mom to stop, I got increasingly upset.

Our grandmother came down the stairs, hair neatly combed and wearing a blue and white floral dress. With great formality, she began lecturing me on my lack of respect to my mother—no glimmer of compassion or faint understanding of our predicament; instead she looked at me as if I were inhuman.

"Bitch."

Heat bulging my neck sinew and veins, my tongue blurted out the curse word to my own grandmother. I had never said that word before, and it frightened me as it leapt from my lips. I ran up the stairs and out of the house into an unfamiliar Lethbridge neighborhood. Eventually slowing down, I walked until my hands quit shaking and the heat drained from my face and neck. I sat down on a curb and waited.

After a long while, my dad came out and told me to come in and eat. Everyone in the house knew what I had said. I was humiliated by my actions. I couldn't look at anyone. Shame fell over me, an enormous grief, a terrible unwelcome feeling of worthlessness. Despite the loathing and the insults, no one ever talked back to my grandmother—not my parents, not my aunts and uncles, not even Grandpa. I had openly crossed over an unwritten code of respect.

I slunk downstairs to the basement and went to sleep, even though it was daytime. Sometime during the day Pumpkin came in and out of the room. I half woke to see her expression, the curled corners of her mouth, her brown eyes wide and shining. An invisible barrier around the two of us very plainly said, "No more." Just as she was leaving the room, I woke up and saw my grandmother's mother, Grandma Hesketh, a kind, gentle blind woman I loved dearly. She came into the room by Pumpkin and moved over toward me about a foot or so off the floor. I had last visited her in a nursing home in Camrose, where she stayed during the week. Her white hair, grayed eyes, and smile shown translucent in the soft light. She told me she was tired and was going to rest now.

I hurried upstairs to tell the news to the family. Sitting on couches and chairs covered with Grandma's fine needlework in the living room and talking quietly among themselves, my relatives looked at me a little strangely. I couldn't blame them. Looking at each of them but speaking directly to my father, I said, "Grandma Hesketh just died."

"What a horrible thing to say!" our grandmother cried, looking faint and hurrying out of the room with several relatives comforting her. I worried about her heart and still felt badly for disrespecting her earlier. My dad quickly suggested I go back downstairs. I was confused—didn't they all want to know of her passing? Dad had taught us about the naturalness of death, and she seemed ready to go. My father and maternal uncles made some phone calls and discovered that Grandma Hesketh had indeed gone.

This was not the last family crisis during this time. A while later, my mother's mother herself suffered a heart attack while visiting us. When we came home from school, the police were waiting at home to explain. My grandmother lived but was so ill that she had to return home immediately. My father's beloved older sister, Velma, died from cancer. Though neither parent spoke a word to us, we knew that Mom was devastated over her mom's frailty. And it was clear that Dad was heartbroken over losing Velma. She was gone, the Helium Research Center was closing, and my dad was growing restless. And so in 1971 my father accepted a position as a working chemist for the EPA in North Carolina, and we moved again.

We journeyed across the terrible Trail Where They Cried and back to where we Cherokees had come from—North Carolina. For months before our return home, Dad recounted stories of the Removal and horrendous division of our ancestral family. Consequently, as we traveled across the stunning beauty of the lands in the east, it seemed as if Cherokee ghosts stood, watching, on both sides of the still unfinished, brand-new Interstate 40. Upon approaching the Blue Ridge Mountains of the Appalachians, Dad announced that we had arrived home. Our ancestors lay all about us in these lands, and we now had a chance for a fresh start.

We settled in between the thickly wooded Piedmont towns of Cary and Apex, staying first in the Knotty Pines Motor Court before finding a house. Straggler ducks and geese who'd fallen behind on their winter way south honked and flapped over the pines and junipers, calling each other to hurry out of there before the hard snows came. We didn't listen to their call, and soon the pipes froze up, but they were so rusted that the hard water was brown, making our hair coarse and sticky. My dad hauled bottles of water from town for us to cook with until the pipes thawed.

It took some time, but we found a place to live north of the tracks on the far edge of town. Our house stood amid pines and dogwoods across Highway 54, about a quarter mile behind the Shiloh Baptist Church. Here, the Black congregation could be heard singing spirituals each Sunday and sometimes Wednesday evenings. Nearby cut a gully where the roads all ended, where water ran across rocks, and where I gathered fallen branches filled with pine needles for weaving baskets and scooped up mud for coiling pottery. Behind our place stood abandoned a cabin built of saplings, our favorite hangout with kids from school. A larger empty house sat quietly and nearly hidden in thick grasses and trees farther out along a line of high wires connecting houses to town. It was a weathered wooden home that apparently was suddenly abandoned—newspapers and coffee cups were set on a checker-clothed table, and dressers and closets remained full, the materials fraying, papers brittle.

North Carolina in the early 1970s was not an easy place to be an Indian or mixed-blood. The region was wrestling mightily and largely unsuccessfully with racial issues. Indians, Blacks, and whites called the state home, as did some refugees and recent immigrants. Scads of military bases across the state yielded mixed-blood families of many races. In another time or place, a progressive diverse society might have emerged from such circumstances and intermixture, but not then in North Carolina. Color-coded bathrooms still appeared in public places; one local doctor insisted that anyone more colored than the shade of paste enter his establishment through a different door; entire beaches were reserved for "White Use Only"; and the KKK openly displayed signs at the edge of some towns.

My father was urgently requested to sign statements for the EPA's record admitting he was Indian (something he had never denied). There was great irony in this because at his first government job his employers had insinuated that the Indian identification should be left out of his application in order to work for them. The EPA lab where he worked was somewhat reflective of more diversity than most workplaces in the state. Indians, Blacks, Asians, and whites worked in the lab as chemists; the administrators were white. When teasing his coworkers when they needed his help or disagreed with him, my father would joke, "All you Eastern Hemisphere people are just alike." His humorous point was a reminder that all of the diverse peoples in the lab originated elsewhere, not in North Carolina, where his blood ran deep. My dad loved his work during this time and creatively flourished.

I handled my new surroundings and peer group less successfully. On one of my first days on the bus, some white redneck kids were picking on a Black kid with ratty shoes named George, who lived way off the main road to the northeast. George was tiny for his age and nice; his face was kind but sticky, mucous plastered his nostrils, evoking the Mentholatum my mother used to cram up my nose. I learned later that those redneck boys had drowned cats down George's family's well and had ruined their water. The old habit of righteously defending others died hard—I rose from my seat, told George to get behind me, called on his tormenters, kicked their shins, and slammed them in the nose. I informed the other kids I'd beat any one of them up if they bothered him again, and a few times I had to. I didn't like the rednecks, and they didn't like me.

Schooling during the 1971–72 school year took place in a monolithic, ghostlike red and white building dating back to the fall of another school and a school before that. Gaping holes exposed the first floor from the second. Plaster and lead paint peeled off the walls in chunks, and the missing false ceiling panels exposed old asbestos pipe and wire. Ticks, roaches, black widow spiders, and sometimes field mice roamed the premises along with the students. We would catch the ticks with our fingernails and run to flush them in the toilets down the hall. Sometimes the yard-duty teachers would burn them between matches until they blackened and popped.

I turned out to be the only light mixed-blood girl in my class that year. The girls I got along with were Jo Ann, Jo Anne, and Vanessa. We all lived far apart and usually only saw each other in school. I was shy in school that year; since I never learned to "white dance" I backed even closer to the wall than usual at school events. I did attend a birthday party for Vanessa, as the only kid not Black invited. I also worked pumping gas and airing tires for Jo Ann's dad at the Shell station (located at the sole traffic light in town), the only kid not full white employed there. I couldn't understand what the rednecks said when they ordered and got things mixed up a lot. Once the gas nozzle slipped out while I was washing a windshield. With the gas spilling all over the car and ground, Jo Ann's father just yelled for me to grab it and clean it up, but the customer called me a stupid breed and refused to pay.

I was frustrated in school because the advanced classes I had taken earlier in algebra I and II, Latin, Greek, Spanish, physical science, and biology were not transferable here because of my age. I was assigned to regular grade-level subjects that I had taken and passed four years before.

Hoping to do something of what I wanted in school, I braved up and registered for a beginning creative writing class. We were instructed to write poems for our first homework assignment. Taking paper and pens out into the woods, past the sapling cabin, I began writing what I saw around me — my dog's paws wetted by water, leaves curling. I remembered Danny, a half-Indian, half-Mexican boy who had appointed himself my big brother when I was little and protected me many times. I wrote about feeling abandoned when left at home on my own at preschool age, about the abandoned houses I knew and visited. I played with the words, tossing thoughts on paper, breaking lines to jumble space. Afterward, I went down to the creek and jumped rocks with my dog. The moon hopped out an hour before dusk, and I went home.

I turned in three poems. One was about water—creek water, drowned cat water, rusted and frozen pipe water, sweet mountain water; another dwelt on misfit kids looking after each other; and the third spoke about vacancies, abandonment, emptiness. Quickly glancing at them, the teacher exclaimed, "Poems can't be written like that! They've got to rhyme at the end of each line. What are these blank spaces between the words? These lines are all different lengths. And what subjects! Don't you have anything nice to write about?" She handed back my paper, asking if I was sure I was in the right grade.

Incensed, I spent the rest of the semester making the teacher as miserable as possible. I turned in for assignments white women's epitaphs, poems decrying Columbus's murderous voyages, and one poem built around my dad's joke about the Thanksgiving holiday as an invitation to dinner where the guests forgot to go home. On stormy days just to spite her, I'd sit next to the windows, lightly whistling an impression of wind escaping through the panes. The teacher would go around and shut the glass tighter, but as soon as she returned to her desk the sound would begin again.

As I entered the teenage years, the relationships among the children in our family changed, for better and for worse. Pumpkin and I developed new ways of working with each other, mostly by ignoring the other's behavior and looking elsewhere for friendship.

We stopped sharing a room. Pumpkin had come home late one night and was experimenting with mescaline, enjoying watching her fingers transform while her friends crawled in and out of the window of our bedroom. I was tired, straight, and waiting for daybreak. When the sky lightened and Pumpkin left for classes, I took all of her belongings and piled them in the southeast corner of our living room. Our father came home that evening, glanced at the heap of her possessions, and, after having a cup or two of coffee, dragged in some framing boards and went to work. A new west wall and north wall with a framed door opening soon appeared; that particular corner of the room boasted two windows and a light fixture so it could easily be sectioned off from the long narrow living room without losing light. Disappearing in his car, Dad returned with a door, hardware, and paneling he'd scavenged from somewhere and completed the room. I went in behind him and arranged Pumpkin's bed and dresser and put a closet pole up for her, straightening everything, making it appear as something special. From that time on we mostly went our separate ways, and nothing was ever discussed about the room or its origins by any of us. (I am certain we have distinctly different memories of this occasion even now.)

My older sister was soon to depart our ancestral homeland and return to her beloved Plains after graduating at sixteen. A Woodlands girl by blood, she still felt more comfortable in open spaces and longed for more stimulating environments, bright lights, and different people. I barely saw her after that time.

Our last time together growing up was spent in another wide open place, full of rolling change and secret sounds.

As I remember, Pumpkin and her friends were partying when they decided to go to the coast one night. She was sixteen then, I was thirteen. She had already seen it once and invited me along; even though it was only hours away and our family drove to Canada on a regular basis, I had never set eyes on ocean water. Without permission from our parents, we slipped away and caught a ride with her friends, spare-changed around for cash, and ended up at the coast at around three o'clock in the morning. Water lapping darkness, waves hitting each other, something popping the surface of the ocean, crabs running beneath our feet—the noise reminded me of inner-ear infections and old stories of great invisible water monsters. Standing on the sand near the dunes, I felt paralyzed and couldn't go any farther until daybreak. I wasn't on anything but was filled with visions of sea monsters and horrible creatures that could come out of the water and snatch us down to the underworld. Pumpkin and her friends walked along the edge of the water under the black sky, not visible but still faintly audible. I wondered if the voices my mother heard sounded like their far-away talk and laughter blowing over the swishing waters.

After the people we rode with left, Pumpkin and I rented a run-down motel room for the weekend. When the lights were switched off, the walls filled with huge black cockroaches, bigger than any we'd seen before, crawling across the plaster and block like nails scraping concrete. Leaving the light on to deter them (a little), my sister and I stayed up all night talking about current political events and wondering where things might lead to next.

My brother continued to react with violence to situations he couldn't control or understand. Just prior to his teen years, he had gone from a chubby kid to a rail-thin boy. My brother then had a love-hate relationship with Mom, who was still having it out with the Buggers. He needed her attention and hated that she wasn't able to be normal. I don't think he ever accepted that she was insane until he was grown. In North Carolina, my brother began to rule the house by beating our mom and me while my dad was at work. Because of her schizophrenia, she believed computer programmers from the federal government were manipulating him. So she never told anyone my brother beat her. She wouldn't even admit it if you saw it happen yourself. No one would believe me, because my mother would deny it so convincingly.

Six weeks after Pumpkin had finally moved out, I discovered my brother beating our mother in the living room. Since he'd chased my friends from the house with butcher knives the week before, I was afraid my brother would kill her. When I tried to pull him off her, she jumped me from behind, screaming, "The Buggers are con-TROL-ling him with ra-di-o waves! They are RAP-ing me! They are con-TROL-ling all of us here! Leave my DAR-ling boy alone! You pimps! QUIT RAP-ing me!" Biting a hunk of flesh from my shoulder, my brother grabbed some pool balls he'd collected and pelted my face with them, yelling in turn, "I have to beat her. That's the only way she'll ever learn! Like you! Like a dog!"

Crying to my brother, "I've learned. I've learned!" my mother continued hitting me in the back, and I was sandwiched. Managing to struggle away, I got hold of a hurricane candle and threw it at them, hitting mom on the forehead. I felt so badly I ran from the house and did not turn back.

I stayed with friends and acquaintances for several months. One night some time afterward, after raging about little things all during the day, my brother self-immolated.

He had been cleaning his bike with gasoline earlier in the evening. Stopping by to talk to him, I clearly remember the smoke curling around the bike from a cigarette in a purple blown-glass ashtray. When I told my brother it wasn't safe to have gasoline in the house while smoking, he cussed and told me to mind my own business. I checked with my dad to be sure if I could stay the night and went to bed after visiting with some friends who lived nearby. Hours later, I was snapped awake by a loud explosion. The smell of burning hair and flesh in the air, I ran out of the room to see the doors blown open and flames shooting from my brother's torso and legs. He looked like a human torch; his jeans, completely soaked with gasoline, had become a wick for the fumes. The venetian blinds shook like breast plates, heat waves rolled like a hot day in August, out in the fields, with an east wind hurling.

With my brother screaming, "Roll me in a blanket! Roll me in a blanket!" my dad smothered the flames with his own bare hands. We both choked the fire around the room with blankets as fast as possible. His jeans did not burn, but the gas was fuming up the inside and outside of the cloth so the smoldering flesh from his legs just peeled off when we pulled his pants down. His right leg was skinned, both legs were burned badly, and he was in shock.

My dad turned on cold water in the tub and told me to get him in it. This was the only time I ever remember my brother telling me he loved me and that he was sorry for everything he had done. I believed him, I wanted to believe he cared, and I tried my best to help him survive. While I was holding my brother in the tub of cold water, my dad called the emergency rescue squad. At first the entire fire department showed up but left without even knocking on the door. Frantic, we called them again, and, while my brother screamed for them to come get him, they argued that it was a joke, that *they* didn't see any fiery explosion. We called another ambulance but were told that we were in the rescue squad area and had to wait for them. No one would listen. It was crazy. Eventually my brother was transported to the hospital, where, after being injected with morphine, he smiled and forgot where he was. Strangely, my dad and I suffered fairly severe smoke inhalation, but my brother didn't.

We knew he had tried to kill himself. There was no possible way my brother could accidentally have soaked his jeans like that, though, confident that our mother's role for me as scapegoat would excuse behavior in other family members, he told the hospital staff I had left a cigarette burning in his room. But my dad and I were convinced that he had poured gasoline on himself, then lit the match — everyone had been asleep for hours, and we had noticed that all the cigarettes had been stubbed out in his room.

My brother was miserable. He kept changing the bandages in front of his friends, eventually getting a bad infection that put him back in the hospital. Calling, he would beg me to come sneak him out, threatening my life when I refused.

I think Pumpkin is the only one of us children who never attempted self-destruction. And she is the only child who ever knew my mother before she went insane. Even to this day I pity my brother. In my view, he always wanted desperately to lead a different life, a life learned from television, school, and mainstream America—a white world, complete with money and a sane mother. But his eyes are the green only mixed-bloods have, and his build is Indian; he needs to see that complexity in himself and deal with it.

Admittedly, at the time I too wasn't grappling well with the circumstances of my life. Besides the usual challenges at home, I felt depressed and sometimes defeated by the lack of educational opportunity and the rampant alcohol and drug abuse at school, worse than I had encountered before. After school, hanging out in the cabin, I started drinking wine with the Bowman kids and other times with Pumpkin's white friend Diane. Walking through woods and fields, or wading in ponds and creeks, we'd drink and talk. I chain-smoked cigarettes out of cartons I'd steal from a highway store in the morning, selling maybe seven packs at school and smoking the remaining three by the end of the day. I was also huffing paint thinner and gas, hanging out in pool halls when I could catch a ride into town. The summer after eighth grade, I ended up using hard drugs.

Where we lived in the early 1970s, young people experimented frequently with hallucinogens and mainlined MDA, heroin, and methamphetamine. Once when we were driving through a nearby town, a young guy held out a plastic bag to my dad, yelling, "You want some peyote?" My dad knew other tribes used peyote for medicinal purposes, so, assuming the offer was meant in a good way, he simply just shook his head to decline as we drove on. While he carefully explained its medicinal purposes to me, I was relieved he didn't realize some people weren't respecting plants the way they should. But, then, maybe he did.

Once again I left home, moving in this time with some of Pumpkin's urban hippie–type high school acquaintances (not friends) who worked at a Dairy Queen on Highway 54. Winnings from pinball and the pool hall allowed me to pay a share of the rent. All of the roomies were addicted to drugs, and none had blood ties to North

Carolina older than their own generation. One played piano like my mom, classical music, all night sometimes. They thought it cool I lived there and were outwardly hospitable to me. Wanting to be left alone, I barely spoke to or communicated with anyone in the house, just checking in to sleep and leaving when I woke up.

One night I got in late, and the roomies were all loaded and painting the entire house's interior as a mural. I joined in, painting animal images, geometric shapes, and faces with anything I could get my hands on—house paint, model car paint. Afterward I noticed near the ceiling somebody had painted a picture of the world and had written, "There is no such thing as gravity—The earth sucks." I refused thereafter to sleep in the same room under this libel of Mother Earth. The slander crept into and evacuated my dreams.

Wanting my own place, I took a job at a Hardee's restaurant. I worked in the back at first, breaking heads of lettuce for salad and turning hamburgers once on the blackened grill (the boss would say, "If you turn them twice it's McDonald's"). I was moved up to cashier after someone called in sick one day and spent months filling customer orders.

While I was working at the front counter, a man with long black hair came in one day and paid a lot of attention to me. When he admitted he was short on the money he would owe for a meal, I didn't ring up the whole order, telling him to bring in the rest of the money later. He agreed and asked what time we closed. Just before closing, I was sweeping up and he came in and paid the remainder of the money he owed. He asked if I wanted a ride home, and I accepted. The man seemed nice enough.

I finished up and met him out in the parking lot. He said he had to pick up something from a house down the road. I didn't think anything about it, saying nothing until we pulled down a dirt road that led only to a pond dam. I told the man there weren't any houses down that way, that I swam down there.

"Let's go swim then," the man urged.

I told him I didn't want to. I wanted to get home. I was tired.

He pulled down the road farther anyway and started talking to me about how he thought I was pretty and nice and that I should "let loose, relax" a little bit and swim with him. In those parts we

61

often swam with our clothes on anyway, so it wasn't unusual to go swimming without being prepared. But I insisted I didn't feel like swimming, saying I just wanted to go home.

He pulled over and grabbed me tightly, his arms wrapping around me like kudzu vines. I felt strangled and did not want to be hugged by this stranger. He tore my jacket off, and I tried to kick him but he kicked me first. Then his hand went over my mouth and nose and cut off my breathing. I remember biting his hand, the man holding me even tighter until he tore off my orange Hardee's smock. I was having my first woman time then, but it didn't stop him.

He hurt me before, during, and after he took me.

Common sounds. A fish popping water on the pond, a splash and gulp. Bats swooping the windshield, crickets chirping every fifteen seconds the exact immediate temperature over freezing minus five degrees. I was slipping into a trance, somewhere off in my head singing, staying away from him—a deer, a wild horse running.

Handing me back my torn work clothes, the man said, "We should do that again sometime." He winked and said he would come see me again at work. After he drove back up the road, I jumped off when I got the chance, and he just sped away.

It seemed on some level as though it had happened to someone else. I told no one, going back to the place where I was staying and locking myself in the bathroom for hours. Sick at heart and full of shame, I called in ill the next day. Becoming increasingly fearful that he'd make good on his sarcastic threat to meet me after work, I called back an hour later to say I was quitting and would just pick up my check, claiming that I'd found another job. I ran away from everybody for days and hid in the woods, stealing food from fields and porches and vowing never to be around people again. One of my friends eventually saw me walking by a pond one day and talked me into coming to live with her.

A few weeks later my mom, having been released again, insisted that she and my father file papers to have me picked up as a runaway. The cops came to arrest me at my roommate's mother's house while we were at a big feed. They burst in like it was a drug bust or something, hauling me away without explanation. I only learned I was a runaway after being processed at a juvenile detention hall all the way down in Raleigh. That's where I stayed, in lockup, until they got me a court date.

My cell was about six by eight feet. A slot in the door admitted a food tray; the walls were solid and so was the cot. Through a barred and wired window, I could see Halifax Courts Projects outside to the northeast. I'd spent some time at Halifax huffing glue and gas, drinking, and smoking up. Most kids growing up there eventually committed a crime and so would come to share my current view of their neighborhood.

I refused visitors. My dad tried to see me, but I felt betrayed. I'd been away for months, so why worry about me now? It was hard to believe he would let her convince him to lock me up without first telling me their plans. I just shut down. On Sundays a do-gooder would show up with a guitar and preach. I only ventured out to see him once. When he began speaking directly to me, I left the room and went back to lockup. I waited the full stay behind that metal door until my court date.

I decided to keep playing guitar once I got out and to write while I was in jail. Sometimes paper and pens were allowed, sometimes not, so whether I wrote on paper or in my head, I wrote. I wrote about drinking and drugs, about being mixed-blood, about everything that caught my attention or that my sister had talked to me about politically: the Wilmington Ten, the Black Panthers beginning to count coup on the KKK at Greensboro, Vietnam, Laos, the BIA, the CIA, Operation Intercept, *Griggs vs. Duke Power*, *Swann vs. the Board of Education*, eagles, and dreams. I did pray—not to get out but for strength to endure.

When I arrived in court, they took me to a conference room where my mother, brother, and the state testified against me. The judge treated me like I was no good, his face pursed in a tight threat and his gavel held as a mere extension of fist. He belittled my testimony, asking if I "honestly expected the court to believe people live like that." Everything I described about the family dynamics was scoffed at and countered by my mother and brother. My dad then took the stand and under oath admitted that everything I had said about the situation at their house was true. After my dad spoke, the judge loosened up considerably and sat back in his chair, arranging his robes.

The court ironically passed judgment more on my family than on me. My brother was sent away to a boy's ranch; my mom went back to the Dorothea Dix asylum. I returned home with my dad and began ninth grade. When, in time, my mom joined us, I left again, this time staying with friends from school.

Ninth grade held the same promise as the preceding year—taking classes I'd passed four years before. Bored at school and depressed, I overdosed several times and once slit my wrists up pretty bad while on crystal meth. My civics teacher pulled me (still loaded) from class and bandaged the scabs without saying anything to me about it. Some of the hardcore guys in the class got together and told everyone (without my urging) to vote for me to be the Science Club president, chiefly, I believe, so we'd have some control over field trips. I did manage to have a boyfriend; his mother let me stay over often, treating me like one of her own kids and even fixing a room up just for me off their garage.

The boyfriend precipitated another explosion and leaving in my life. One day I came back to his mother's place; she was pacing the kitchen, pointing at his room, shaking her head, and making gestures with her mouth and chin that something was up inside there. I opened the door to his room, caught my boyfriend with a girl named Star, and walked quietly out of the house after giving his mother a hug. The boyfriend put forth every excuse imaginable, from studying a scene for drama to modeling for photography class, and begged me to understand. I refused to discuss it with him and intended to simply walk away from the incident. The indiscretion seemed par for the course for the boy and provided a convenient excuse to leave him. Unfortunately, Star confronted me about him at school the next day and pushed at me with her arm. The shove pushed me over the line. I wasn't upset about the boy, but no one I could take down ever pushed me and walked away unaffected. I jumped Star and beat her up in the nurse's room, blacking both eyes.

Expelled from school, I left the state, breaking probation by doing so but wanting again to be by myself. I retreated into the woods and mountains, canoeing and camping, mostly up on the northwest side of Buffalo Gap but sometimes toward the south. Being alone in the mountains was peaceful, and no one bothered me much. Cherokee blood relatives (though we weren't in touch) were within reach if I truly needed help.

When I finally ventured down into the Piedmont, I began living on the street, sleeping in Laundromats, abandoned cars, or in the ditch—wherever. Toughing things out. I also started hanging out in places where music from Papa John Creech and Mississippi Fred Mc-Dowell filled the space between walls. The pickups Papa John put on the f-holes in his violin sparked a sound more electric than Eveready. Bottlenecks on steel strings made me feel like living.

Such music brought breath, but it brought out creatures too. One time I went to a Leon Russell/Billy Preston concert at Charlotte, hitchhiking down with a friend. We decided to drink coffee at a hotel. When I went over to the counter to ask directions to the concert, the clerk mistook me for a band member and handed me keys to a suite on the top floor. Acting like the gesture was expected, I told them I'd go up when we returned from the concert.

During the concert, some white people discovered Leon Russell's new wife was a Black singer, and they practically rioted over it. Many got up and left, leaving more room for other people to come in. The stadium was full; drug busts were going on during the show. Bikers working as bodyguards threw people off the stage as soon as they climbed up. A cop got shot or stabbed right in front of us. We couldn't hear his screams but saw the blood pouring while the music continued and thousands of arms waved to the music, undulating like an eel's nest.

After the concert in the top-floor hotel suite, I ran into Billy Preston in the hall. I was trying to buy a pop out of the soda machine when he came over and opened a huge ice chest packed full of wine, beer, and liquor. Preston invited me to come on down the hall and join them jamming, so I did. Not easily impressed by people or situations, it was no harder for me to join them than to attend the show. I ended up leaning against a wall listening to them play, imagining the fans as carnivorous plants like giant milk pitchers leaning toward the stage and eating anything that came toward them too quickly.

About a month later I went down to Fayetteville to see Joe Cocker. He never sang much, just leaned back and moved to the music. He was so loaded they had to carry a trashcan on stage for him to throw up into before they dragged him off. I attended the concert with three friends, one of whom had an older brother who drove us there. After the concert, the two brothers decided we should go over to Fort Bragg, where they had played when their dad was stationed there years before.

We hung out there on the shooting range that night, getting tuned up, playing war. My friends decided to take a walk, but I remained on the sand dune, alone, watching the brilliant expanse of stars overhead, much as I had always done with my father. My friend Tony's older brother was singing a song.

The song died quickly on the wind. The older brother was behind me suddenly—close behind me. He put his hands on my shoulders and pulled me down, grabbing at my jeans and hissing to be quiet. I fought him, but I was loaded, and he overpowered me easily. My "friends" came back and saw him advantaging me. They shouted for him to stop but didn't try to intervene.

They were on my right side, watching him assault me; I was still trying to stop him, and the sand dug into the small of my back—

Base helicopters flew overhead once, twice, full of men, and I imagined they could plainly see what was happening below. Overpowered and helpless, I disassociated, looking beyond the helicopters to the stars shining all around and above. The same stars brimming with my ancestors' cosmology and my father's stories taught me now how truly insignificant every moment on earth might really be, how one day this moment might be nothing. I focused completely on the North Star and began to sing in my mind songs of deliverance and of the better world.

When the older brother was done, he pushed me down the dune and walked away. My "friends" apologized, claiming they'd beat him up one day when they were bigger, combing my hair away from my face and assisting me back to the car. We all rode together, my attacker driving, his eyes alternating between the road and the rearview mirror, watching. Nobody ever said another word about it. Neither would I.

SELF-IMMOLATION

His Levis laced with gasoline
so thick wet legs became funnels.
No, wicks, in a holocaust.
Skin turning into hard ash.

"Roll me in a blanket."
"Roll me in a blanket."

Screams from the burning
board floor.

Windows blown out.
Doors blown off.
Flames blowing, blowing,

"Roll me in a blanket."

I threw one to my dad.
We smothered charred legs.
We smothered the entire room:
walls, doors, window frames,
bed, and bike

dirt bike, 175 Yamaha.
He was cleaning it with gas
and stealing one of my smokes,
a Winston filter.

I peeled his pants.
The meat came with the denim.
We placed him in ice water,
bones exposed,
muscles barely hanging.

The only time he ever said,
*   "I love you."*
*   "I'm sorry for all the*
*   things I've done."*

I believe it now,
decades later.

The smoked venetian blinds
shook in the wind like breast plates.
Scorched ticks swollen up like grapes
full of blood
climbed the cheap paneling
trying to escape.

Like me, he'd tried to take
his life.
Like me, we both survived.

4

Ashes

I have often heard that near each positive a negative lies waiting to attach itself. And, often, when faced with undesirable realities we are forced to make decisions. Sometimes, depending on our personal situations and perhaps because of the plain biophysics involved in life and living—even though we may want better and much more positive end results—these decisions may end up as choices between bad and worse.

I began to hate staying still. Beginning during the year of my ninth grade in school in the early 1970s, I hitchhiked around from town to town, county to county, rez to rez, and state to state, sometimes staying with friends and relatives out on the Plains. That winding trail, sometimes fulfilling, sometimes treacherous or dangerous, almost always sad, left me bruised and wiser. Always, in time, that trail of ashes would lead me back home, back to my ancestors' land and my father, and then it would call me away again.

Once I'd just gotten back from a Forty-nine following a Pow Wow when two of my sister's acquaintances wanted me to drive a 1962 Bel Air they'd "borrowed" because they were too loaded to drive it. Although pretty tuned up, I handled the tank just fine until a semi rounded a corner at an intersection on the dirt road we were taking. I hit the brakes and nothing happened, no connection, no drag—nothing. We hit a tree head-on and V-shaped the entire hood and engine. The passengers had black eyes and were in shock, and I lost an eyelid but wouldn't get in the ambulance. We hitchhiked to a hospital and had the eyelid repaired. The doctor, who was named Noah, warned me I would have to be extra careful for the next few days—branches might snap at my face if I walked in the woods, and if I blinked a stitch would pop too soon.

My dad invited me to recover at his house; I agreed to stay a while to appease him. My mom was home for a short stay but would be going back to the Dorothea Dix sanitarium soon. One day I placed the sheet music of Leon Russell's "Me and Baby Jane" (about a heroin addict's demise), then "Going Back to Alcatraz" on the piano board and asked my mother to play. She did — flawlessly — singing with such irony the songs suddenly seemed fully realized. Her conscious mind was twisted, her memory shattered forever; she couldn't even tell her own kids apart from others, but the music was always there. Musical scores embedded in her fingertips rather than memories, my mother played on, celebrating chords and melodies that had eluded the damage the psychiatrists had done.

Death seemed to be a companion on my trail during this time. Several weeks after returning home, I was a passenger in a vw Bug that hit the rear end of a Cadillac while going sixty miles per hour. Crashing through the windshield and through the Cadillac's back window cut me up badly, and I was badly bruised, sprained, and stitched from face to legs.

I also nearly died while having my wisdom teeth removed. Obsessed with my "Indian teeth," the oral surgeon talked about the scalloping behind my teeth that white people don't have and how dentists and doctors can tell mixed-bloods by bones and teeth alone — no matter how light we are. He seemed to take his knowledge seriously while explaining he had trained at Indian Health Services straight from dental school. He could also tell I had lived in the Oklahoma/Texas panhandle area for a while because of the excess fluoride deposits on my teeth. I felt like I was the subject of an anthropologist's "premortem."

I had never had local anesthetics since the age of three and was quite used to singing in my mind as my father taught me to do during all dental work, stitches, and simple medical procedures. The oral surgeon, however, insisted I receive Novocain for the surgery and loaded me up.

The shots burning, the surgical saws slicing away my upper wisdoms, I think of my brother having skin grafts. The oral surgeon's face transforms in some way, and my face swells so big I can see my

own cheeks. I touch my head and feel it enlarged with fluid. There is
pain in my chest before I am given shots of adrenalin and Benedryl,
and I hear words on a phone to an emergency room, "I think I'm
losing her."

I remember and see.

Pumpkin and I singing, we were maybe seven and ten,
decked out in black and white robes covering our worn-
out homemade shifts, singing in Latin. Pumpkin had stolen
the communion wine from under the altar, and I had spent
practices signing to another kid who understood sign and
kicking in songs in Latin upon the director's cue. Our mom
had made us sing in this choir. She would rarley set foot
inside the church herself, too many gossipers there to judge
what everyone else wore that day, too much organized reli-
gion not to provoke paranoia of additional plotting against
her, too much to anger her, too much for her to bear. She
warred with the Buggers in the parking lot while we sang.

We are singing now in Indian and lying outside in calico
dresses high on a hilltop facing Grandfather Mountain. The
flowers are all blooming around us, and people are dressed
in the old way. My dad's people walk over to us, and I turn to
grab Pumpkin's hand but she vanishes along with my grandmother. All these people come for me but vanish before I
reach them. I'm in the mountains, high in the mountains,
there seems to be no below.

Pumpkin is in our living room watching a movie about
the Mayflower, and both of us mimicking our dad yell at the
pilgrims, "Wrong shore! You're lost! Go back!" Hoping with
each yell a boat would turn and take back all the pilgrims
just so things would be different today.

I'm five again and my parents are broke, and my mom
tells me the sheltie my dad gave me at birth is going on a
trip. I'm eight and realizing she sold him, kept the money,
and he's never coming back. I'm nine and huffing glue. Not
all the time but more than enough. The glue makes your

head go numb. It feels like you are in an impermeable reverb chamber.

I was back in that reverb chamber when I came around, my head looking like a basketball and my heart taking several weeks to beat normally. I didn't want pity from anyone so I ended up staying again for a couple of weeks with my father. I couldn't do anything for myself, and my dad was good at helping without making you feel helpless. There was a song called "Basketball Jones" on the radio that Pumpkin would sing to me over the phone, teasing me because of the swelling.

I'd already missed almost all of ninth grade, so the near-death experience didn't affect my schoolwork. In fact, I stayed out of school as much as I could, first landing a salesclerk position at Sears over in Raleigh, then waitressing at a restaurant adjoined to College Inn motel in Raleigh. The restaurant was nicely decorated, with tables covered in deep red cloths and portraits hung along the walls. I was working eight-hour shifts for sixty-five cents an hour, plus tips, on a child's work permit.

One time an actor in a popular television sitcom came through Raleigh with the play *Pippin*. He sat at one of my tables with another man and, after learning we didn't serve ice cream soda, demanded I go out and purchase the ingredients to make him one.

Getting tired of his attitude and I'm-a-star syndrome, I asked, "Haven't I seen you somewhere? You look familiar." When the actor bragged about his television role, I nonchalantly replied, "Oh, I don't watch that shit." The actor called over the manager and had me fired. Afterward I picked up some fast food work and other waitress spots, but they were fill-ins and didn't last long.

I returned to ninth grade after being out of school for so long and promptly saved the life of a girl named Wanda Bobbitt in science class. Wanda, an even-tempered, tall, thin, medium-complexioned Black girl, sported a medium-length afro. Her hairdressing caught on fire one day when she leaned too close to a Bunsen burner flame. Straightening up, her entire head engulfed, Wanda was paralyzed, her eyes caught in headlights. Bolting from my chair, I grabbed the teacher's coat from a hook and instructed the teacher to hold the coat around Wanda's head to make sure it was smothered.

My quick action guaranteed that no matter how many school days I had missed, and how many assignments I had failed to complete and turn in, I would be permitted to take the ninth grade finals. I passed into tenth grade, earning A's and B's on the final exams, which brought up the incompletes and missing papers to C's and D's.

I spent that summer picking beans, digging potatoes, working horses, and doing other odd jobs. I needed this work. It rooted me, cementing a connection to the land that would deepen in future years. The fields were so green you felt plantlike at the end of the day. I was also exercising and green-breaking horses for pay and doing fairly well getting work this way. Unfortunately, every time I ran into someone I knew, they'd want to take off hitchhiking somewhere to drink and I'd go along and end up missing work. Summer ended sooner than I wanted, but even though I really only had an eighth grade education I was hopeful for the next year in high school.

A few weeks into my tenth school year, the white principal called me into his office. Closing the door and taking a swing at me, he accused me of selling drugs on campus, something I had never done. The vice principal, a Black man who was the only school administrator you could talk to if you were in trouble, came in and pulled him off, threatening to hit him himself if he raised another hand. I left, not even taking time to clean out my locker. Later, I took some night school to catch up, fully intending to get a GED, but I couldn't always get to class and my plans began to disintegrate.

Amid such misunderstanding and machinations, I didn't have the heart to be around anybody anymore. At the age of fifteen, I began hitchhiking throughout the southeastern United States, eventually heading in search of the blues to Macon, Georgia, a destination chosen off of the back of an album cover. My mind was filled with music, the sound of bone and bottle on steel, of lip and breath on brass, of lives calling out in song. I wanted to be there. I wanted to climb right into the middle of black vinyl and spin in the heart of tone, in the keys of an old Steinway, in the bluest blues, into the blue calling—

Mapping out my traveling route by those gas stations that served free coffee, I made good time and hit the edge of Atlanta around the same time the national fifty-five-mile-per-hour limit went into effect. A billboard of Bo Didley banked the highway near where I napped up high in a crevasse underneath a concrete overpass. Bo will watch over me on this stretch of road, I thought, while checking the hawkbill knife in my pocket, sliding down the concrete, and sticking my thumb out to the next car.

Two guys picked me up, and I climbed into the back seat. Ten minutes down the road they asked if I was packing.

I didn't answer.

They then asked if I had any weapons at all.

Remaining quiet and looking for a level stretch of road to dive out of the car, I grabbed hold of the chrome door handle.

A click followed by a blade in front of my face. The knife was at least six inches long and jagged on one edge, the other side filed down to a clean rim.

"Here," said one of the men nonchalantly, flipping the switchblade around the other way. "Here, have it." The men also tossed me back a couple of fresh packs of Marlboro reds and warned me to be more careful when accepting rides.

Thank you, Mr. Didley.

My ride into Macon was Susan Bear, tough looking, talkative, and involved with the Allman Brothers Band. Having hitchhiked herself into Macon years before, she was concerned about my age. The number nineteen popped out of my mouth; she scrutinized me for a second, then went on talking. Eyes filling with tears, Susan spoke of Duane Allman's recent death, of how much she had loved him. She said she could imitate Greg Allman's voice almost perfectly and began singing "Ramblin' Man" while driving me to a halfway house where I could clean up and eat and stay for free until I could become self-sufficient.

The roomy and old halfway house had two stories, a wooden frame, tongue-and-groove clapboard, and a wraparound porch. In exchange for food, soap, and towels, you had to help out cleaning and cooking and also talk at the dinner table. The drawback was the constant attempts by the owners to convert you to their version of

Christianity. I stayed there off and on until the first frost, when I rented a skid on College Street for fourteen dollars bimonthly.

While living skid, I ate only what I could steal; any money I made went for drinking and rent. When returning to my room, I sometimes tossed the winos on the stairs of the building a half pint, and they settled down quick enough. I was content—the passing days fell like sheets of rain, and I didn't have to answer to anyone anymore. There was no press for time, so the details of my surroundings intensified. I blended into Macon on a gut level, a part of the physical environment but not of society. It took time, but I stopped running and began living again.

Now needing to get out around people, I found Susan Bear at Grant's Lounge listening to a band called Birnum Wood. She let me bus the tables and bar for tips. It was a hot place; while bands like Wet Willie played in the back, one of the music companies, maybe Columbia, scouted there. I spoke little, partly because I was always wary they'd discover my real age and partly because I didn't really know the women or feel I could trust the men. My pool game was mean, especially combination layouts, and my Rook and Spades were deadly, so I soon made plenty of free drinks off bets. I drank full-grown men under the table and beat many of them at wagers. Sometimes the bartender would line up shot glasses, and people would dare me to outdrink a challenger. I have no idea how I drank as much as I did in those days.

I started hanging out with bands, sometimes as a roadie, sometimes jamming, singing, or just relaxing and taking it all in. Birnum Wood took special interest in me, and the Indian guy in the band, Gary Redwine, lectured me about the way I was surviving and urged me to quit drugs and alcohol and respect myself. Most of the band's women were good to me, and they had me out to eat several times. Many of the band guys were protective, regarding me as a good kid who needed to be escorted home at nights. Most who walked me home were nice enough, making sure I was safe.

One bodyguard type, standing six foot four and weighing around 280 pounds, however, proved different. Once we reached my place, he threw me flat on the hard floor and held me by the neck. I would like to tell it differently, to say I tossed him aside like a foam rubber pillow, but there was nothing I could do; my blades were safely tucked away under the pillow across the room. I wish I could claim it never happened, that I never allowed anyone to do anything to me—ever! But I cannot. My mother's screams as we took her to asylums—"They'll RAPE ME!"—echoed in my ears, and I now wondered if it had been true, if the attendants had actually raped her when she was undergoing shock therapy, if she had been going through this all along and no one knew.

Not wanting to face people after what had happened, I left Macon without a word to anyone. I hated to leave. I loved my place and the music and thought of Macon as a home of my own, a place where at last I fit. I just packed up and started walking. As my steps carried me away, a man played a blues harp on the corner. His mournful song tucked itself into my brain and still plays sometimes. I had never heard it before that day and will never again.

With perhaps two more months of cold weather remaining in the new year, I decided to look up Pumpkin, who'd been accepted at a college back in Amarillo, Texas, where we'd been born. Thumbing through Alabama and Louisiana, I was picked up on the second day out by a family man in a van. After showing me pictures of his wife and kids, he drove down a dirt road and tried to rape me. That man was fat, bigger than I was, but small for a man. I fought him while his family's pictures looked on, pink smiles and clean faces staring, stopping me from using the knives I carried with me. He did assault and molest me, but I managed to keep from being raped again. Afterward that husband and father panicked, drove to the nearest town, and stuck me on a bus to Memphis, saying, "Be careful," like he knew and cared for me.

While hitchhiking through Arkansas, redneck kids in a schoolyard next to the highway stoned me. Pelting me on the head and face with rocks, they continued hitting my back even after I had turned around. A trucker picked me up just as a cop pulled over behind me. He claimed to be Sauk and Fox and that he and his wife took in runaways; I told him I was on my own and didn't need nobody.

At sundown we pulled into a roadside cafe, its front covered with painted ranch brands. The trucker insisted on buying me a meal. I ordered grilled cheese, because it was the cheapest thing on the menu and because my stomach had shrunk since I was using. I wrapped the leftovers and put them in my jacket pocket for later. Renting a room for me to sleep in at the motel next door, the trucker said he would be waiting across the road in his rig come morning. True to his word, he gave me a ride all the way to Oklahoma, where I visited some friends at Tulsa, Tahlequah, and Oklahoma City. I ran into a cousin on the Leatherwood side at a dance and found a couple of Walker relatives nearby.

Each time I found Oklahoma relatives, the stories my dad told of our family being split up during the Removal became more real and poignant for me. It was good to meet relatives I should have grown up with, but the joy was accompanied by a certain sadness underneath. None of my Oklahoma cousins had ever seen the Smoky Mountains, never swam its rivers or watched the leaves color. I couldn't imagine what it was like to live forever so far away from the place of our heart.

I called my North Carolina probation officer — collect — feeling guilty for not having called in sooner. She was a nice white lady — honest, patient — her face badly scarred by acid thrown by a probation kid. Mrs. Wren was concerned, her voice comforting, saying she wouldn't send the cops for me but that I did need to keep calling her and to come in when I was back in the state. She had been with me in spirit since I was in juvenile court from the Halifax Courts detention center. Even though I knew she cared, I didn't know how to handle it. Telling her I would stay in touch, I let the receiver drop and never called her back.

Come the first clear day, I headed down to the Panhandle to find my sister. Amarillo was not familiar, since the town had grown considerably over the years. On that day it had snowed in the early morning, and by afternoon the temperature hit sixty-two. I found Pumpkin's place after asking around for hours and hours. I waited on the concrete steps by her curb, smoking Winstons and writing a song on the inside of the cigarette pack wrapper.

Pumpkin appeared, accompanied by a white guy. They glared at or through me, walking right by without speaking. A few minutes later Pumpkin came back out.

Looking me over, she asked, "You looking for someone?"

"You don't know me?"

A suspicious raising of brow betrayed no hint of recognition. I couldn't believe she didn't know me and smiled at her a little.

"Allison?"

"Yeah. It's me."

"What are you doing here?" Pumpkin demanded, sounding more pissed off than happy to see me. She was thinner now. Not the half-chubby kid I remembered but still dark and beautiful. Both of us had hair way past our hips.

Pumpkin seemed to be my last chance to get off the streets. Although she didn't want me, I convinced her to let me stay for a week or two and get checked out at a clinic. Sporting callused tracks and collapsed veins, I was emaciated and so tired. It was a tense, unhappy time for us all. Pumpkin had me do her household chores while she worked but didn't want me associating with her friends and generally acted ashamed of me. I reasoned that, if I could show Pumpkin I was useful, she wouldn't mind me staying. At the Safeway supermarket, I stole a couple of cartons of cigarettes and some hamburger and bologna while she shopped, never noticing a thing. When we got back to the house, I showed her what I had gotten. She grabbed the meat and started yelling that it was a felony to steal meat in Texas and that she wasn't happy about my shoplifting. She and her boyfriend fought about little things all day, her dog seemed paranoid from all their bickering, and the couple of cats she kept in a closet behind the bathroom acted frustrated and panicky, frequently jumping at the bathroom window, crying and pouncing on the pane. I identified with those cats; their leaps at the window mirrored my growing helplessness and desperation.

Pumpkin took me into a free clinic, where I was given some medications. I had some type of blood infection and other ailments, for which they loaded me up with an antibiotic shot and pills. Afterward she called our parents and said she was going to put me on a bus back home. I didn't want to go, but I knew better than to try to argue with her. I would never win.

Back home in North Carolina, my mom was in full glory, her ongoing commentary and ranting now focused on Watergate and impeachments. My dad talked to a boss at Fairmont Foods in the then newly grown two-light town of Cary, North Carolina, and got me a line job packing crackers in the factory. It was union work, so I earned over minimum wage for the first time in my life. I had no idea what a union was, so failed to pay for membership and consequently was almost ganged in the factory parking lot before finding out.

On the graveyard shift, I worked next to a drum filled with peanut butter. Bright orange crackers were lifted off the conveyor belt by two stackers who'd place them in the packaging unit; peanut butter then would be sandwiched between the crackers, and they would come out the other end wrapped in plastic. My job was to slide ten packages together off a belt into a cardboard box ten times until it was a hundred count, seal it, and then start again without missing a beat. If the crackers were badly wrapped I tossed them into a box for hog feed. If I missed even one package it could slide off the end and would have cost me my job.

We weren't allowed to leave our sites for any reason, though we could turn on a light for any mechanical help, machine repair, or an emergency with the crackers. There were two ten-minute breaks and one half-hour lunch break, and all the women were supposed to eat, drink, and hit the bathrooms at the same time, meaning that someone usually got left out of the bathroom and had to hold it for eight hours straight. Austin Foods didn't miss a beat—the entire break room consisted of tables and retail-priced vending machines full of Austin products. For years I couldn't stand the smell of peanut butter or watch anyone eat it. Until this day, when I pass through a town with a cracker factory, I can identify its odor over every other pollutant.

I was using and dealing with my friends, but the cops and local sheriffs sold more dope than we did. Drugs were everywhere. Even used car dealers were fronts for dealing, concealing the transactions by turning to card games when the busts came down. We believed everyone selling in those days was somehow connected to the organized crime rings that were shipping drugs through North Carolina to D.C.

and New York from Florida. The head narcotic agent in our area got busted with marijuana plants growing in his living room. It was me who made the call to the 800 number listed in the phone book, "Report a Dealer," placing the call from a pay phone so there would be no trace. I figured that since these guys were sworn and paid to uphold the law they should be the ones to go down first for breaking it.

The people I hung out with did not play; life in North Carolina in the 1970s was serious business. Cops paid off snitches with drugs, so, being addicts, they would report their best friends and brothers for a fix. Some of my acquaintances killed each other over drugs. One white guy from my sister's class was burned alive in his own home, tied to a couch, over a bad drug deal. That same boy had once lifted me high above his head against a brick wall outside a pool hall, choking me while leveling accusations of stealing drugs from him, which I knew nothing about. He was working on breaking my arm, twisting it up and hard behind my back, when a couple of other mixed-bloods from Charlotte came up behind him and beat him up before getting me out of there. Another guy I had gone to school with had gotten cleaned up, married, and was holding a newborn baby in his arms when he was shot point-blank over a bad deal from years past. Another was forcibly drowned.

One weekend I ran into a white girl from school, the daughter of the police chief, who invited me to come stay with her at a place down a dirt road between towns. As soon as I got there she shot me up with some MDA. I soon screwed up at the Fairmont Foods job, quit, and lived the entire next year in a shooting gallery. Inside my new home lived four couples and me. I was definitely a loner and slept by myself in the living room by the woodstove. While they all had their own bedrooms, I had the stove and the company of cold dogs and cats, as well as their fleas and ticks. Before the hard freeze, no amount of dope seemed to deter the ticks. They dug in during your sleep, feeding on blood, until they swelled like grapes. The FBI had our house under surveillance. Helicopters and small planes flew by with infrared at night, and during the day cameramen could be seen hanging out the sides of the craft, shooting.

I was down to shooting up in my wrists and legs. My elbow pits had collapsed veins, and the skin was hardened into calluses as thick as plastic so that you couldn't drive a needle through. Shooting up six to ten times a day, I ran drugs and picked up MDA and heroin in Pemberton, Greensboro, and Charlotte, at houses guarded with machine guns by guys fresh out of Nam.

I bought needles by the case at the drug store by the highway, somehow passing for a diabetic. When the points dulled I would sharpen them on a matchbook like honing a blade on whetstone. The house was surrounded by sheds and shacks from its farm days, which we filled with aluminum beer cans and used hypodermics. We saved so much aluminum we bought a car from hauling it in for cash at the scrap yard. The pond out front was used for fishing, for stashing newspaper machines we robbed for change, for dumping purses the women in the house stole at Laundromats (I couldn't bring myself to steal from individuals but did continue to shoplift), and for cooling cases of beer let down into the cool water in steel milk cages tied by rope. The pond debris was so plentiful that it served as bedding refuges for fish and turtles. You could have built a bridge across the pond with the cans, needles, and evidence of thievery lying around.

No one ate much food. We were all on liquid diets. Morning would bring a craving for alcohol so bad I'd strain cigarettes from half-empty, leftover beer cans. Going through the house and collecting stacks of cans, mostly arranged into pyramids during drunken stupors, I'd take a bowl or pitcher, hold a pan strainer across the cans, strain ashes and cigarette butts out of the warm leftover beer, and drink it for breakfast. For nicotine, I'd pick up butts in ashtrays and meticulously unroll each one until I had enough secondhand tobacco to roll a smoke. I would smoke a carton every two or three days if I could get them. When the weather turned cold, three or more feet of snow and ice winds blowing, anyone who had some cash could hire me to walk to the store five miles away through the woods by adding me in a pack of smokes to their order.

Though by all rights I should have been beginning high school like other kids my age, I now spent my days traveling from the junkie house to drug pickup spots to the pool hall—where I picked up extra money on pool wagers—and back. I eventually started playing pool down on Hillsboro Road in Raleigh, always shooting a twenty-one-weight stick because my backhand was a little shaky. Combinations were still my forte. An old man, Black, grandpa-like, whose name evades me now, showed me trick shots, and I teamed up with him on Fridays to hustle the urban college boys. We would split the proceeds and buy rounds to keep in good favor.

My second severe allergic reaction occurred during this unhappy and confused time. Because I mainlined, my blood was checked at the clinic fairly often. I learned I had contracted the clap through sharing needles. The clinic nurse gave me a shot of penicillin at the clinic. Feeling a sensation of hot lead shooting into my hip and leg, I informed the nurse about my previous allergic reaction to Novocain. She advised waiting around thirty minutes before leaving in case of a reaction. Nervously I sat in the glass-walled clinic with blue vinyl chairs (which reminded me of asylum furniture) and pamphlets on whatever virus was going around at the time. After forty-five minutes, I left and drove home.

On the way back everything went black. Somehow making it to the driveway of the house, I laid my hand on the horn repeatedly for help. People kept yelling, "No curb service!" as a joke but did not approach until the cop's daughter came out, riddled with fresh tracks. Telling her I was dying too fast to do anything about it, I asked the cop's daughter to look after my dogs and cats and told her where I had stashed a twenty-dollar bill behind a light switch plate in the living room. I didn't panic but simply accepted my situation and surrendered.

She managed to get me to the hospital, where they used a heart massage on me. I remember everything—the shots of adrenalin and Benadryl, the jumper cables, the nurses acting so excited over it all, the doctors talking as if I couldn't hear anything. And I was looking down at myself, knowing I did not want to go back into that drug-infested breed body, feeling so free, so full of peace. Voices were telling me things, singing; I could see grass and trees in front of me, and I wanted to go. I dreamed and could see once again.

I am eleven, only four years before, strong, healthy, and seeing what had happened by a creek off Iron Mountain Road in the Black Hills. A beautiful creature stands in front of me, a doe whose eyes are filled with trust, sweet and brown. I reach down to pull some grass. She raises her head, my hand putting forth an offering toward her soft muzzle. Chewing, she nuzzles me for more, her nostrils taking in sweet mountain air, scents of flowers blooming, even my eleven-year-old girl scents.

The doe's mate watches her from my right, occasionally showing off his rack, rocking, pawing the dirt. She's still standing knee-deep in grass, waiting for me to feed her more. I continue to reach down, pull more tender blades, and offer them without speaking, without expression, except the smile I put into my eyes when she looks toward them. He then comes forward, the first time a buck has approached me in all the times I have fed doe deer in the Appalachians, in Glacier, Waterton, and throughout the Rockies.

Reaching down, I pull younger sprigs, yellow-green, and put them to his mouth, keeping my eyes down and hoping he will eat. He grabs the grass quicker and more firmly than the doe, as if tearing the blades from the ground still. As he munches loudly, the green running down his muzzle and foaming a little, I offer some sweet berries. The doe moves in and bumps me to be remembered. Feeding them, I wish for a fawn, so that their whole herd would come out from the trees and I could stand among them offering grasses, roots maybe, and kinship.

And then I am riding with some of our cousins about an hour west of Spring Coulee in the Canadian Rockies. Weighing forty-nine pounds in seventh grade, no horse minds my burden. I am long-legged, and grownups say I am built for riding. You can live on horseback if you want, I believe. I see Pumpkin riding, but my brother is held back by our mom and put on the slowest horse. His white horse looks tired, its back worn to a curve and eyes almost blank. I jump bushes, creeks, and draws while the others ride closely together. I am mesmerized by the contrast of the forest green and my buckskin's tan neck and face; he is stunning. Soon the horse

of one of my girl cousins won't budge, so I make a big deal
of riding it back at full run to the corral, waving for a couple
of guys to follow me. I give those guys chase, they probably
thinking that someone had died the way I ran him, jumping and leaping whatever we could along the way. When my
brother dismounts, his old white horse falls over dead.

The doctors shock me back, and I leave again, fighting for freedom. They pull, I struggle.

Eight years old, I am messing around in my parents' room.
My dad has a box containing rings, pins, and other things
he has collected, some from World War II, the rest from his
family. His father, Grandfather Vaughan, had left him a gold
railroad watch, originally picked up secondhand around
1912. Grandpa had worked as a machinist in a Santa Fe Railroad roundhouse during World War I in La Junta, Colorado, where he got the watch. He had learned to speak
Japanese so that he could serve a second shift as a pusher or
foreman, sixteen hours a day, six days a week, for a couple
of years straight. Grandpa had taken an examination for
field artillery and was promised the commission of second
lieutenant but had asked for induction delay until Auntie Lucy was born. She was born November 4, 1918, and
World War I ended on November 11. After he left the roundhouse, he carried the watch for the remainder of his life.
Grandpa Vaughan was born in 1878, died in December 1949,
but he's here.

I swing this watch on a chain, pretending to be a zoot
suiter. The watch spins, Dad behind me reaching out, and
the link breaks, ruining the watch stem. My dad takes the
watch from me, hurt by my carelessness, but just putting it
away quietly and asking if I was done playing in there for
awhile.

I am now older, ten or eleven years of age, and hear my
father's voice dimly through a dream of running, fleeing a
man bent on killing me. A dream often repeated, by some

buildings I'd never seen before. Somewhere surrounded by pines.

I hear my father, and, rising from the top bunk, I grab Pumpkin's shoulder and nudge it, saying, "Get up. Come on." And she does. And my brother. And our mom. We go to the back door, quietly following my father's lead, and look through the glass to find the sky alive with millions of falling and shooting stars. When I spread my fingers, it seems as though the spaces between them are filled with lights.

The doctors say, "I think we got her."

Animals press around me, everything I ever took down and all of their unborn. They're letting me pass through them, nudging me along, through the grasses. I'm passing through their furred and feathered bodies.

I don't question anything, not needing to. I turn over on a hospital bed and open my eyes.

During that year I also nearly died by someone else's hand. One night I was holding money for a large deal and stashed it in the couch. A new guy, who bothered me for some reason, was visiting and saw me hide the money; I cut eyes at him advising he leave it alone. The other people in our house said he was okay, and one had done time with him before. This new guy, Greek, John, ended up playing guitar with us all that night. Later that evening he offered to boot me up. I extended my wrist toward him, and he hit me with what was supposed to be MDA. I watched the blood draw and vein check; the syringe was clear, but there was no strobe, no swirling, no heat flush characteristic of MDA.

Cartoons began to flood the walls—Donald Duck, Road Runner, Quick Draw, Sylvester—the strips were live action and fully animated. The entire room ebullient, after an unknown amount of time, I rose, knowing you don't hallucinate like this on MDA. He had shot me up with something else—LSD, STP, exactly what I didn't know. A partial plate to replace a lost front tooth was gone from my mouth, and my hair felt like tangled cotton candy all dreaded out.

I made it down the hall and into the living room by feeling my way past the animation, trying not to touch Daffy's webbed feet or Donald's orange bill. The couches were filled with people watching TV, who seemed to look right through me. I tried to talk and an inhuman sound came out, low and dragged into a slurriness.

Was I a ghost? I touched a guy I knew on the shoulder, begging for help with my eyes. Looking back at me with a strange look, a look like you give a baby, he asked, "You in there?"

I nodded and he got up, took me into the kitchen and asked what I remembered. Grabbing some paper, I tried to write that I knew it wasn't MDA this guy had shot me up with, but I couldn't remember being left- or right-handed and had trouble holding the pen. Increasingly frustrated, I attempted to talk slowly to make the words phonetically form sound at a time.

I got it in my head that I needed to be shot up with some MDA — what I was used to — in order to get me high so I could come down from this other stuff. I signed and motioned for him to shoot me up. Although he looked like he really didn't want to, I was insistent.

I felt nothing. No strobe. Nothing.

Again, I motioned.

And again.

And again.

About the sixth mainline I strobed, throwing up, which was normal, and the heat rush was there.

It took all day for me to come down. I learned later that a contract had been put on me for dealing too much dope in someone else's territory. Being such a kid, I didn't even know lines had been drawn. The new guy shot me up with a full gram of pure PCP, which should have killed me. I was in and out for six weeks, conscious and unconscious, a zombie. At some point I even tried to brush my teeth with a shaving razor and almost choked on my denture plate, so my housemates took it from me. I apparently wouldn't let anyone brush my hair, so it had fallen in dreads when the other girls held me under a shower every few days. The women assured me they'd protect me and kept me with them all the time. But because everyone was strung out, they didn't risk getting busted by taking me in for medical attention.

I also found out that the new guy, whom I had immediately distrusted, was the same man who had met me at Hardee's and had raped me. I had blocked him out entirely upon second encounter.

The next week I signed myself in for voluntary rehab for speech therapy. My voice sounded like a muffled horn. It took me a while, a long, slow while, but I regained most of my speech. I still stutter on occasion, but no one can say whether it is a result of that or another experience. When I feel myself going into a stutter, I talk with my hands, drawing out everything I say as I speak, manually pulling the words from my mind through my mouth.

The junkie house eventually burned to the ground, by whom and for what reasons are unknown. After the house was gone, most everyone who lived there left the state. The police chief's daughter stayed and got married. I attended the wedding, interestingly enough held in the police chief's home, with cops and junkies both seated on the bride's side. My brother had been involved in a recent bank robbery, and they were looking for him. My mom was sick and didn't know anything about anything, yet they were bothering her all the same. I handed a note to the chief during the wedding stating that they should leave my mother alone. He nodded, and nothing else was said.

Although adrift and constantly wrestling with self-destruction, my understanding of and involvement in the world continued to deepen and widen. In the early 1970s a lot of people my age were becoming aware of pressing social problems and found unacceptable many of the values of the last generation. Some big-city Skins connected to the American Indian Movement appeared, spreading the news locally about what had been accomplished with the Alcatraz and BIA headquarters occupations; it was the fifth official year of AIM, the Alcatraz takeover had occurred two years earlier, and Wounded Knee's occupation was ongoing. Some Indian families I knew on the Plains were still going through relocations, being shipped off to Chicago and Denver and moving around as much as I was. Those still at home mainly wanted just improvements in order to live better. I did whatever I could where I was living, participating in rallies and demonstrations, fighting cops and rednecks, and mailing letters and calling to lobby and support other Skins coming through on fundraising tours. I was fifteen and believed I was grown. Looking back, I realize now that most of my efforts went unnoticed. I ended up usually tear gassed or clubbed up while making bread in kitchens.

North Carolina was not sympathetic to social progress then. Cops strung up Indians and Blacks who were politically active, labeling their deaths as suicides. Tensions between the Black Panthers and the KKK simmered in Greensboro. A number of nonwhite locals were beaten by cops at concerts or when driving through KKK towns past dark. Even wannabee Carolina-version hippies, like those Pumpkin had sometimes associated with at school, avoided crossing redneck lines. Many towns were not hospitable to me or my friends; it was risky to drive through them at night or to rent a motel room or apartment there. Cops and shop owners gave me a bad time almost everywhere I went. I felt that they hated me because I was light yet proud of my Indian heritage and because I publicly hung out with Skins, other mixed-bloods, and Blacks. Sometimes when my friends and I ate in diners, waitresses or proprietors would threaten me or put pubic hairs in my food as a warning. I was the one who heard all the racist talk—the things bigots were sometimes afraid to say to darker complexioned individuals. The real hatred. What they said behind others' backs was thrust in my face, a face that must have been a constant reminder of racial mixing.

I began working at a store, making honest money. I hooked up with a working guy who used to come by pretty often. He was mixed, too, and panther looking, sporting long, dark-brown hair and eyes, a moustache, and a sweet mischievous smile. Stan was eight years older than me, and his dad was a Bible thumper, a deacon or something. (I should know, but I wasn't raised that way and never can keep the positions in churches straight.) His father didn't approve of young people setting up house without a legal marriage. Consequently, Stan brought my dad some field corn. They talked only a short while before Dad filled out the paperwork required for someone my age to marry. We held onto it for the future while we made plans.

We were both looking for a better way to live and decided to leave

Dad (on left) and his brother
Sam during World War II service,
February 1946

Mom after World War II while
attending McGill University

(*Above left*) Pumpkin (*right*)
and me, 1959

(*Bottom left*) Dad and me, 1969

Travis and me, Newport, North
Carolina, 1980

Pumpkin (*right*) and me, San Francisco, California, 1986

Mom, Santa Paula, California, 1988

Travis and Vaughan, 1989

Mom, Dad, and Pumpkin, Santa Paula, California, 1990

the area and seek work elsewhere. We hitchhiked to Greensboro, where Stan had some friends, but jobs were scarce. He took me to shopping centers and had me spare-change us money to drink and eat on. We got by for a while, but cold weather was coming, and neither of us liked being in town, so we went up above Cherokee and camped out, living on fish and small game.

Being back on the reservation was good for both of us. No cops bothered us, and we felt at home, much safer than down on the Piedmont. The slopes of the great mountains cradled us, and we loved the beauty of the leaves firing up the hillsides with fascinating colors. Neither words nor paint could duplicate this glory. Oftentimes I'd run into people whose names I knew to be relations and we would visit, after which I would sharply remember and miss my aunties and uncles.

Winter came hard that year. Our tent, buried under feet of snow, was kept warm by a kerosene lamp. We washed our hair in river water heated on a Coleman stove. Although we were very cold, pouring heated water over our scalps warmed us so well we could get down to T-shirts comfortably. There is something about the water in those mountains, something that softens your hair and skin and tastes so good that you want to swim in it, even if it's frozen on top. We mostly ate rabbit, birds, and dried meat.

That time in the mountains was the happiest for me since I was young, and I didn't want it to end. I wanted to stay. The d.t.'s came and went, but we stayed off alcohol the entire time we were there. I was still using MDA, but it was too cold to shoot, so I placed it under my tongue when Stan wasn't looking.

Eventually, we realized that we both needed to work. With few job opportunities nearby, we headed south, hoping to work by picking fruit in a warmer climate.

We stopped overnight in Macon, a place charged with memories for me. People in Grant's Lounge recognized me and came by our table. The bartender lined up shot glasses on the bar for me to down, just to see if I still could. Stan couldn't believe all that I had done in my short life. I'd tell him something and he'd say, "bullshit." Each time people vouched that I had been somewhere before surprised him. In Arcadia we were walked through town by police who flatly despised hitchhikers. Stan and I then picked oranges for some southern groves and made around four hundred dollars before it was time to move on.

At one point in southern Florida, we got picked up by some crazy white drug dealers who said they were traveling from St. Petersburg to Key West on a haul. A huge German Sheppard was in the back seat with us, growling the whole time. Sitting between two guys in the front seat, a girl poured drinks and lighted joints while the men fondled her. Looking in the rearview mirror at us, the driver said, "We love hitchhikers," and then slammed on the gas, speeding so fast that the speedometer stuck and the doors shook. There was no point in jumping out, since we'd die on impact. Knowing all too well the power of windshield glass on facial skin and stiff bones, I wanted to be limp, to be Jell-O, and quickly went to sleep.

The next thing I knew, the people in the front were fighting among themselves and telling us to "Get the hell out!" They pulled over to the roadside briefly, and we hopped out as fast as we could, trying to appear undisturbed. Stan and I began walking. It was by now dark, and all around us came sounds from creatures moving in swamps. About a half-hour down the road, we spotted where our last ride had left the asphalt and wrecked. The passengers looked to be alive but in miserable shape. A car had stopped to render aid already, so we kept walking. I remember the German Sheppard going back and forth among the wounded, licking their faces.

It took three days to get a ride on Alligator Alley, the highway bisecting Florida's Everglades. Tourists were being robbed by highway women at that time, so no one would give us a ride. Stan and I were so hungry that we ate cream of chicken soup straight from the can. It tasted like shaving cream. After three days, an ex-con picked us up and drove us to Miami. We headed north, deciding we'd do better back in North Carolina.

Our next ride claimed to be the black sheep of the Maytag family, showing his tattoos, telling us to dump our cigarette ashes on the plush carpet of his luxury car, and even giving us keys to a houseboat where we could get some sleep and clean up.

We continued north and returned to North Carolina. We decided to try to get work in Southern Pines, one of three towns forming a triangle of the heaviest golfing area in the state. Beautiful land. Good soil. Grass green, so green it boggles one's concept of color. Stan still held on to $380 of the $400 we had made in the orange groves, enough to rent a house, pay a deposit, buy enough potatoes and flour to live on for a month, and get the lights turned on once we moved in. We rented an older place next to the tracks.

I immediately got a job waitressing at the Southern Pines Resort, making good pay and tips. I was the only waitress not Black, but a couple of the Black waitresses had Indian in them, so I wasn't the only mixed-blood. We teased around a lot and enjoyed our work. The all-white golfers liked nonwhite servers, so it was actually easy to get work there. Looking into the serving area from the kitchen was like gazing at pure, undiluted whole milk—white men, white women, white boys, white girls, white bosses, white owners, white companies, white babies, all wearing white clothes. Most of the foods were expensive ones I had never eaten. The tables were all set with cloth and silverware. Sitting on the tables until the food was served were large metal, maybe lead, plates engraved with designs relating to the restaurant and region. It seemed strange that these large disks had no specific use other than to occupy space in a place setting until a plate of food was served.

Once DuPont people sat at one of my tables and ordered meals and drinks. They kept ordering, and I kept running after their orders, happy and treated well. When they were leaving, one of the DuPont men handed me a $100 tip, which he claimed was for my smile. Including my other wages and tips for this one night, I cleared $185. Since Stan had hocked my electric guitars while I was at work once, I decided to use this additional money to get my own things in order.

Stan and I headed northwest to get my dogs from my dad's place. I was paranoid about Stan's reaction to my mother's insanity, but he just shook her hand and spoke respectfully as if it mattered not in the least. This was the first time in my life I had witnessed someone other than my dad being able to look at my mom as disabled without judging her. I was overcome by an immediate sense of safety in his company, and my dad accepted Stan by inviting him to help work on his car outside.

That evening I called my dogs, a couple of young setters and a sheltie I'd had since I was eight, and we left. The dogs adapted to

Southern Pines just fine, staying on the porch and minding the home whenever I was gone. At night they would go around and steal clothes off lines and milk and newspapers off porches. When I woke up, they would show me all the presents they had brought. Once I came home from work and the dogs had trapped a wino from the tracks on the porch. Crying and begging to go, the wino said they dragged him up by his sleeves. I gave him a pack of cigarettes and a sandwich and apologized. I was forced to leash the dogs afterward, although I hated to.

Apparently excited about my setters and sheep dog, Stan spoke of his two pointers back at his parents' place near Willow Springs. He started talking about the two of us settling there, growing food and hunting together. He also began suggesting that I should quit using, an amusing request since he used himself. He insinuated I was an addict, and I retorted belligerently that I could quit anytime I wanted. At the age of fifteen, all someone had to do to get me to do anything was to dare me. That's what happened—it was that simple. He dared me, so I quit.

I went to work without hitting up and made it a couple of hours before having problems. Going home early, I doubled over, convinced it was a miscarriage. Stan kept checking on me and waiting to see if I would figure it all out. I was convinced it was some female problem and made him take me to a gynecologist. The doctor confirmed I was in withdrawal—cold turkey—and in for a ride. I hurt so badly that singing in my mind was the only way I could tolerate it. I refused the methadone services and toughed it out, figuring that if I was going to stay off the stuff I probably needed to have a worse taste for it than I already had.

Sometime during the night—I'm not sure which one or even how many there were—I had a complete myoclonic spasm that took all my muscles to premature rigor mortis. I felt like a windmill turning in an ice storm, no, molten rock, no, ice, sheets of ice clunking up against each other somewhere. My limbs became switchblade steel, welder's torches, ice picks.

I took flight in my mind, escaping that torment, that bitter fifteenth year, of ashes and addiction. I swam upward, biting something so hard I cracked my incisors on the left. I was up and out and covered with water. Then everything stilled.

The People received prophecies about great fires engulfing the pioneer-and Civil War–ravaged lands. These fires would purge the earth of the whites, cultural and environmental despair, and everything would be as it once had been in this rebirth. People remembered that each step on this earth is a sacred motion, movement, and exchange with our own mother. A mother who provides everything we need. Some began cultivating corn, squash, and beans and refrained from drinking to dedicate themselves to the strengthening of the family. Many complied with the government on a surface level, some lied to the census takers about their racial identity, to avoid the ever meddling white man. These were the dark ages of North America. The People were hungry; they were without. The most important task at hand was to ensure survival of the culture. They began to use passive resistance. Willows in hard winds.

5

Back to the Lands

Deep metallic thuds wake me. I am lying on blue foam rubber rolled
over flattened Nash seats, my thirty-dollar Rebel Rambler pulled up
tight between thick willows bordering the stream and a Visqueen-
covered plant bed. It is morning, more or less, somewhere around
4:30 a.m., the time dew hangs on mustard greens and fog fills field
furrows knee deep. The stretched Visqueen imitates lake ice, but the
humidity is definitely growing season.

William, an old man I work with in the fields, waves a steel thermos at me, grinning, a thin man with a face creased from smiles and
weathered from working and much drinking in the sun. William is
Stan's uncle by marriage. He always comes to wake us before the others get to the field.

Rolling up the foam, I pull the seats upright, comb my hair, and
step out of the Rambler canopy. Upon standing I light the last Winston in my pack, knowing I'll roll Bull Durham or borrow from the
old man's Pall Malls the remainder of the day. I puff quickly, hot-
boxing the smoke, and accept the steaming cup of coffee offered.

I look around for Stan, my half-side. He is usually checking the
beds by now, lifting the plastic sheeting to find how many seedlings
are big enough to set out into the field. The old man bends the brim
of his red cap into a more prominent fold, confiding, "He's already
gone for the tractor." His wife and several other women come out
to work, their heads wrapped in bandannas, dresses hanging shin-
length over pants and aproned. They raise their chins at me, and I
meet with them over by the stand of willows, the smell of fried eggs
and toast lingering on their clothing and hair.

Stan comes around by the spring, wearing a green nylon-mesh ball
cap, his dark hair hung in a long ponytail from underneath in the
back. He hands me some dried meat and a sweet potato cake, and

I give him my refilled thermos cup of coffee. His mother and sisters arrive in a white '52 Ford pickup. The girls aren't far from my age, one older, one younger, both pretty, with hair down to their thighs like mine and Indian faces tucked away behind large-framed glasses and scarves. Suspicious of our sleeping accommodations, their mother scrutinizes the drying mud tracks behind the Rebel's wheels.

We go to work.

The men pull back the plastic sheet and join us women down on our knees pulling plants with the certain gentleness necessary to pre-vent bruising or breaking of the tender stalks. We work with a loving-ness toward the plants. The tiny green tobacco, barely larger than a hand's breadth, is ready to take to the fields, to be placed on clamps, hand over hand, clamps spoked on a wheel behind the tractor, spiked into freshly turned earth piled in mounded rows as far as you could see before the trees rise and join the horizon.

1975. I was sixteen years old, my birthday a half season away yet. In a few weeks I would be settled down, married, sharecropping. For a time Stan and I had stayed in Southern Pines, for a time in Raleigh, though neither of us could stand living in town long, so we'd often end up sleeping outside, waiting for paychecks, just to be together and to stay away from town. For the last year we'd mostly lived in the car, hunting in winter, fishing in summer, and following work in the fields. Eventually we settled into a North Carolina sharecropping house, clapboard and tin, wringer washer and wire lines stretched out back, heated by woodstoves in winter.

The families had agreed, and Stan was eager to take over fields of our own. The two of us had worked together side by side in the fields and migrated for work through a few other states as well, seeking crops to pick—beans, potatoes, tobacco, lemons, whatever was ripe and ready for harvest. We'd decided to settle together back in North Carolina, at home, where all of our southeastern Indian ancestors had always been.

Stan's family had sharecropped 'bacca for generations, but this would be my first time; although I'd planted and picked by the day, following the growth in the fields from county to county, I'd never had a chance to make decisions about the work. With Stan's family, we would work their Willow Springs allotments and have ten acres of our own to plant. If we made good this first year we could pick up additional acreage from the surrounding landholders—all white men—on fields so rich from Indian living you still turned arrowheads up with each furl of the plow.

Now that we're gathering a few roots of my story, let me tell you just a bit more about Stan. He could be talkative, mainly because I was withdrawn at the time, and he was strong—although standing about five foot nine with a twenty-eight-inch waist, his chest measured forty-two inches across and his arms were huge from working manual labor. I still remember the gross sizes because I sewed everything he wore back then except for T-shirts and blue jeans. We were both mixed-bloods—his mother was Indian, his dad was white—without tribal status, and bore the pain of taking urban jobs when the fields went dry. Stan was a Vietnam-era vet, and he'd driven racecars at Rockingham. He rebuilt engines right in the middle of the living room without getting a drop of oil or any grease on the floor. Stan taught me how to "take curves" and "side wheel," and practically every driving trick I knew I learned from him.

Stan was not a bad man; looking back he was one of the hardest-working men I've ever known, but he did have some problems. When driving at night, sometimes he would think someone was after us and would drive with the lights off so "they" couldn't see us. I never saw anybody, but I did learn to drive in the dark fairly well—you can see trains coming a lot easier if your lights are off in the first place. Stan's paranoia, perhaps related to his war experiences, almost always erupted after a night of drinking or hustling pool, especially if he was smoking weed. His chimera seemed minimal in comparison with my mother's schizophrenia, so I adapted to such situational intrusions on our relationship without much worry.

The sun rises as we move from one plant bed to another. Again and again, the men raise Visqueen, exposing green leaf on black soil, and we work throughout the morning gathering tobacco plants strong enough to survive transplanting to the fields and replanting them. We give in to the rhythm of fieldwork—the steady bend and rise, the motion of tending new growth, opening and closing spaces in the earth, creating patterns, united in the movement, much like communal dance during celebratory and ceremonial times. There is a glory in this motion. It often caused one to sing out loud, and sometimes the singing was so great the mighty sun felt as if it gave way to the beauty of the sound and burned a little easier down upon us in the rows.

Come midday we break for lunch and drink lemonade from a tree someone had brought up from Florida just to see if it would grow. This tree is covered during winter snows or hard freezes and keeps putting out lemons each year, dreaming it is still in Florida. Its spring blooms are waxy and thick compared to other trees nearby, a stranger welcomed all the same for the good lemonade in the summertime. Sometimes we make sun teas and lie in the shade of a black walnut tree left in the center of a field just so the primers could take a shade rest in the middle of the day. It's an ancient tree full of nuts so hard you have to freeze and pound them with a hammer to crack the shell, nuts that make ice cream and bread delicious. Sometimes we'll lie in damp grass, pull back Visqueen off the earth, and lie on the mud, hoping to cool our hot bodies.

Just below where we work, next to the fields where we will transplant these seedlings, lies our own garden, more than an acre whole. I'd tilled the entire field weeks before, driving a red and gray Massey Ferguson tractor when the moon signaled planting. On other mornings, just as early, my hands are low down in hills of early peas, my eyes devouring each and every young pod long before they are ready to eat, still stiff and without swell. A few days before, I'd torn one off and eaten it whole, the bite of green pod refreshing and tart, and that particular taste now fills my mouth when I pull tobacco, remembering pulling wild plants that would choke out the garden once the row grew too thick for hoeing anymore.

Every plant, each herb or food, in our garden is grown by its neighbor on a barter system, each row planted to assist the opposing rows with their own growth. Beans produce nitrogen, corn plants need nitrogen, marigolds bordering the southern side repel insects that eat up leaf, squash and pickling cucumbers run the northern edge just below the tree line, mint keeps the ants away, and so on.

Earlier we buried fifty-gallon drums to their rim and filled them with composting materials, covering each with metal lids painted black to absorb the sun and speed up the process. By the time the fourth drum was filled, the first would be ready to mix with manure for fertilizer. After the plants passed a seedling stage, I kept no scare in the field to ward off birds—so they helped pluck insects off the plants, bees hived an old tree not far away, and I released each mantis or ladybug I could catch into the garden. It seemed every bud must have pollinated because later that same summer the garden will out-grow any other for miles and miles. There will be so much growth that I will eventually make arrangements for surplus sales with spe-cialty food stores in towns within driving range. But even this early in the season, when fog and leaf, gray and green, swallow the earth completely, I know there'll be plenty.

We return again, midday, after the hottest hours to prime and work, hitting each row and claiming the leaves for our own, with at least four men on either side of the tractor and a female or two alongside and driving.

The day grows hotter and hotter in the tobacco fields, the stretch of heat waving shoulder high on the primer just ahead, the same on the one behind. The heat waves bring rhythms and patterns of their own into those that come directly from priming leaves and tuck-ing them into elbow crooks until the space between your arms and body exists no more and you are carrying fifty pounds or more of fresh green tobacco, searching for the trailer to lay them in, only to start again and continue for as long as the fields run and the heat breaks.

Every minute in the field something green is appreciated and honored. On such a scorching afternoon I am brought by the field rhythms to certain praise, to pray for rain and to sing to bring it on. My father-in-law tells me to knock it off, since he doesn't appreciate us singing in Indian out in the fields. But when the rains come he is glad too, though he will not admit it. When it pours, sometimes we leave to do other things and sometimes we continue working, en-joying the cool wetness on our backs, then stopping to rest and visit together at sundown before walking back to our houses and cars.

In the evenings, the motion of fieldwork lingers away from the fields; even in our sleep we still prime, continue taking each leaf around the bottom for half a stalk, reaching in circular motions to grasp all four in a single round. All night while we sleep the leaves are laid into a trailer and taken to the barn to be looped on a looper run by older women and overseen by big men who have grown too old to prime the fields anymore. The trailers are full, green leaf brimming the sideboards and humped up over the carts like a train car carrying coal.

Come morning it is all real again. Halfway through the night we are up checking tobacco barnburners. The women underneath the barn bind the tobacco by string to sticks to hang in the barns in layers, and layers of rows of tobacco hang like saddle bags on some crazy stick horse charge. By 4:00 or 5:00 a.m. I return to the fields and drive or prime or loop, catching shy smiles and sideways glances from hot primers but giving my own only to my man working hard every bit of the way through the fields.

As we prime the tobacco field rows, dressed in tar-covered shirts, faded jeans or khakis, and baseball caps, crop dusters sometimes soar overhead while spraying the fields, usually with malathion. Occasionally a pilot will get his kicks by spraying us with his cargo.

I'd worked all day in the fields one particular sweltering day in July and had been doused by a crop duster the same as everyone else — not the first time for me. At the end of the row where jugs of water were placed, I poured a few cups over my head as usual to get the smell off from the spray and kept working. After bathing that evening, I bedded down, feeling a tingling on my skin. Beginning to wonder about the sensation, though exhausted from cropping, I fell into dreams quickly and stopped second-guessing.

Horrendous burning.

I leaped from bed, yelling for Stan to help me, around two o'clock in the morning. Tearing off all my clothes, I stood in front of him shrieking. My skin had reddened and rose until 98 percent of my body was covered with huge splotches, splitting and oozing. Stan tried to wrap a bed sheet around me, and I screamed for him to take it off, unable to even stand the touch of sheet cloth.

Stan pulled the truck up to the house and helped me in. I desperately avoided touching the seat with my body and tried to keep the sheet as far away from myself without showing my nakedness. Fires flared in my memories: my brother incinerating himself; the curing fires burning in the bottom of the tobacco barns; flames from last winter licking in the woodstove; fires from camping out in deep winter over on the ridge; fires from cooking drugs on stainless spoons; and sacred fires burning in pits and hollowed logs and inflaming our heart of hearts still today. I understood that my fire was a part of all those that had come before, but bringing neither reason nor comfort now, just scorch.

It took the hospital emergency room over an hour to determine that my condition resulted from chemical poisoning in the sprays dumped on us in the field. I will never fully understand why I was the only one who reacted so violently to the spraying. It took weeks for me to recuperate, and for years afterward, when I smoked, a small hive would appear on my bottom lip for no apparent reason. I began rolling my own tobacco from plants in our garden that were never treated chemically.

Only a few days after I'd fallen ill, I was back in the fields, itching so badly that by midday I just stood in one spot, shaking.

Come late season, rain would commence around three o'clock so often you needn't wear a watch to clock the day. The rains provided good excuses for fishing. Sometimes we'd break from the fields, wait just till the lightning died down, and then hurry down to the ponds, hoping the rains disturbed the fish in a certain way to make them hit a hoola-popper, beetle spin, or purple worm. Sometimes, however, what would bite after a rainstorm were freshwater eels, two or three clustered on the same treble-hooked lure, twisting and turning, angling themselves around with a certain strength and strangeness — blind eels where you couldn't tell head from tail, provoking the same uneasiness as gigging a snake. If you sliced one in half, would it be able to grow two ways like a worm? We ate them if they were the only catch at the time, but we were also likely to cut them loose, Then they would prowl the waters again, sliding effortlessly across pilings, beaver dams, stumps — whatever blocked other creatures from crossing. At night, up around the banks of stumpy, black water ponds where we gigged for frogs, beavers and raccoons sometimes visited or debated territory, leaving footprints along the banks for everyone to see come morning.

When we gigged for frogs, one person would ride in the back, rowing and steadying the boat, while another sat in the front, armed with a long stake fixed with a forked spear for gigging. If possible, a third person might ride in the center, wedging a shotgun between their knees and a flashlight or lantern to scope out and still the foot-long bullfrogs we'd gig, perhaps also holding a fifth of liquor, jar of bootleg, or T. J. Swan. The center rider also helped to sight moccasins and cottonmouths hanging over our heads from swamp trees reaching out of the water. Water snakes make you quiver in a way that commands a special sense of respect, a sense of eeriness—unexplainable, unquestionable—as if by mandate of the very waters they dwell in. Snakes four or more feet long, patterned and thick as your arm. Heavy. Snakes with a distinct heaviness that bedded all over those ponds, nesting so thick an unknowing swimmer might dive in young and healthy but float to the surface dead and covered with snakes. These snakes would slink down tree limbs and into our boats; as we scrambled to gig and hold them out over the water, the center or back rider would cut the snake in half with bird shot or buckshot.

It's one of those summer nights when the moon contests a ripened pumpkin. Stan works the oar, kerosene lamp, flashlight, and gun while I sit up front with the gigs only. No one else is around, but my man is more than capable. A fat bullfrog sits stunned and Rayovac-blinded on the jut edge of bank; I spear and lift him into our boat—the twelfth that night—and our bucket is almost full. Stan asks me to toss a line in the water and jitterbug for a while. I reach back and, grabbing a Daiwa rod, sling out a cast toward the bank's pocket. The second stroke brings a good-sized small-mouth, the third another. We gig two more frogs. As we head back, the loons begin to sing. Back home, Stan axes the back legs off the frogs, leaving them crawling around on their front legs looking confused and trying to ignore death, like the chickens Auntie Velma wrung when we were kids. Stan pours salt on the severed legs, and they begin to jump as if feeling the burn long after their bodies crept away. I pity them. It is hard to witness, so I pray for their little frog spirits, thanking them for the food they will give, hoping they understand somehow.

We need meat. Frogs, fish, deer, bird, rabbit—we eat or sell whatever we catch and grow what we can't find wild. The skins from every four-legged creature we down go to a useful purpose, as do the feathers and even bones. We eat cow guts and tail soup, and even heads and other parts are gobbled up by the dogs and cats. We always pray for good days, clear nights, and clean water for healthy kill, for survival. Mostly we get what we pray for, and we never take a small frog or one singing as we pass by.

One thing for certain about a teenage girl who works hard in the fields all day is that she is not one to reckon with on her birthday, particularly a girl who has never liked that anniversary, possessing too many bad and sad memories surrounding that date. I turned seventeen at the end of that sweltering summer, and Stan presented me with a brand-new broom and toilet brush. I laughed at first, thinking he was poking fun. Realizing he was serious, I got so mad I went to the kitchen and, picking up my best frying pan, a black cast-iron skillet, reeled back and slung with every bit of field muscle my arms bulged. Stan ducked, the pan crashing into the wall edge on hard wood and splitting neatly in two. Furious, I gave chase, but he hopped into the truck and took off before I could catch him. Stan came home late that night with his arms full of fresh-cut flowers, some bright printed cloth I'd been eyeing in town, and a mess of fish in a new pan.

The next day Stan took the split pan to a neighbor who worked in a welding shop some distance away. When the welder brought the pan back he hauled a truckload of his coworkers with him to our place so they could see for themselves the less-than-ninety-pound girl who broke a cast-iron pan in half. In the kitchen, I was busy sewing the cloth he'd brought me to make up, pretty amused about the whole thing myself. I remember the look on the coworkers' faces when I stood up, them eying my biceps and calves like they'd never seen arms and legs before.

I loved to cook. In the kitchen, where I spent most of my time while inside our house, I sewed and quilted, baked and fried bread, canned vegetables and jellied fruit, made homemade candy, split nuts, butchered meat, and cleaned fish. In the refrigerator, along the door shelving hollowed in places for eggs and butter, right next to the butter space stood rows of oleo wrappers. A wooden, gate-legged table filled the center of the room, and fresh cobwebs neatly crossed the ceiling corners. I adored that simple room.

I can't remember a time when I didn't have some project going in that kitchen. When I wasn't quilting I made dolls; in the fall I would gather dried corn husks and fashion them into dolls, using dried stalk as a torso. Sometimes I took them with me to stomp dances to give away, and sometimes I'd just give them to our relatives later, during the wintering months. If I wasn't working on cloth or husks, I wove baskets or blankets on a loom or painted or made pottery.

I was still writing but not showing my work to anyone. One of my friends from junior high moved near us and told me she had always liked my poetry. Convincing me to gather some poems together, she typed them up, "just to keep in case you want them someday." Those poems were like shucks I'd used to make husk dolls or the first circle on a basket weave. I created, then, my own particular patterning in song-story, revealing a mobile generational patterning.

I tried to, but just couldn't stop traveling. Maybe I should have thrown away my shoes. I'd always worn a pair until they wore completely out before buying new ones; maybe these shoes just had too much traveling memory in them and wouldn't let me stay settled. Perhaps I should have thought to set some strawberries that spring. I loved them so much, and it is common knowledge that the Great One made strawberries appear in Corn Woman's path to keep her from leaving First Man long ago, thus preventing what could have been the first story of divorce. Maybe I could have jellied and put them up for winter preserves alongside scuppernong, plum jams, and watermelon rind pickles in the freestanding cupboard, along with the roll-up cabinet, side-bin flour sifter, and dough board.

Soon after my eighteenth birthday the next year, when we sold our 1976 fall tobacco crop, I put a down payment on a brand-new 1976 Ford F100, my first new vehicle. Stan had insisted, claiming that the first thing to do with a lump sum of money is to get some wheels that will last until the next pay, truck wheels that will carry you to work in winter through iced fields and snowed-in back roads. I picked out a metallic evergreen truck with a white topper on the cab and green Ranger interior. The truck resembled so closely the color of sunlit pines you could slide right by a pond on a white farmer's land, pop a hoola-popper or beetle spin in, scoop up an old granddad with a mouthful of leaders, and fish for a long time undetected.

Two months later I drove Stan up to Canada to meet my maternal grandparents, driving all the way while he slept and stared out the window. Crossing Minnesota, no cars or even semis shared the road with us; strange, but I kept driving through the night. Crossing the border at sunup, I stepped out of the truck and slid about a good twenty-five feet on black ice. I'd been driving on that ice all night without knowing it. In a town near my grandparents' place, we drank rye whiskey, smoked Player cigarettes, and visited around places I'd grown up seeing. I drove Stan up to Calgary and Banff, then southwest near Waterton, where my mother had grown up. As I drove I remembered tunneling through the snow to feed my grandpa's horses when we were kids, and I felt at home here too. We then headed farther south to visit some more.

Although the roads were blocked through the Tetons, I got out and moved the signs, laying cinder blocks in the pickup bed to add weight, chaining up the tires, and then driving through. It was so beautiful—Old Chief Mountain within sight, the surrounding lakes frozen blue. Later, Stan and I hit Browning and stopped at the same café where my dad always had paused to eat bread and drink coffee. Upon the surface of our coffee, like green clouds on lake water at night, floated the same iron flakes I remembered from childhood visits.

After seeing my relatives and friends all over the Plains, we headed down to Arizona, where it was legal to drink at seventeen. We stayed drunk with mutual friends there for a good week before heading up to Oklahoma to see old friends and Auntie Rose.

Stan suddenly panicked, threatening to jump out of the truck if I didn't head back east. Apparently he believed that if we didn't go back to North Carolina now he might never see it again. I explained that we *were* going east and that Auntie's was close to being on the way. He jumped.

I pulled over, got out a beer, and walked over to him. "You okeh?" I asked.

He looked pissed. "I mean it," he declared. "I'm going back now."

Handing him the beer, I explained, "Don't be so bitter, we're just visiting around. I did this every year of my life with my dad, and I'm used to it. It's just something I need to do."

He wasn't convinced.

"Okeh," I continued, "I'll take you back. No problem. I'll just call Rose and tell her we can't make it."

I wanted to call her and explain that he wasn't used to traveling and wasn't handling the road very well and I was going to take him home. I wanted to say something to my friends, being so close and not able to at least visit them, but I couldn't.

Until we got back to North Carolina, we only stopped for gas and supplies. I was confused by Stan's fear. I knew he was a vet during the Vietnam era, same as all my male cousins too young for Korea, and had traveled during his army years, so I wondered how he'd made it in the army if only two months of visiting was so difficult. I began to suspect that he was shell-shocked, though it didn't seem like a crisis situation to me.

It was midwinter when we returned. Restless, I rearranged each room in our house, moving around the buy-on-time and yard-sale furniture until everything looked different, exchanging bedroom curtains with living room drapes, pulling rugs from room to room, taking guns and fishing rods and hanging them on walls in the last room before the back door. The tin woodstoves were hot, filled with chopped wood from dead trees we felled and cut up with chain and bow saws. I began spending more time in the only unheated room—a built-on room for summer entry with a trough sink for washing out our field clothes and peeling off layers of tar stuck to our skin from 'bacca. Now I stood watching out over the fields, through the woods, entranced by red evening skies striped with purples, the sunset so intense it was almost unbearable.

I know I never worked against this marriage and was without guilt or blame, but now things began to change.

Stan went back into construction work, and I got one job training and caring for dogs and a second job counting pharmaceutical pills at a drugstore in Raleigh. It was ironic to now be counting pills legally for pay. Since I was already in the city, I also began taking night classes at NCSU.

One night in class I got a call that Stan had been injured. Driving home, I found him waiting with two casted feet, the result of a fall from a scaffold that had broken. He was in a bad way and wouldn't be able to work for a couple of months, so I was glad I had work to carry us.

With him home all week we spent more time together than we usually did in the off season. On weekends we might go out to a juke joint with some friends from the fields. The juke joints were surely the hottest spots around. We mostly sat around visiting, getting to know more about each other than we ever had before. We drank less beer because he wasn't out driving but consumed more bootleg brandy because it was closer to come by. Sometimes we'd get some bootleg with lead chips, but I'd drink it anyway and hallucinate for a whole day from the poisoning. Other times the bootleggers would mix up some special peach brandies for colder seasons, drinks that were prized and smooth as sunsets.

Stills were everywhere in that part of North Carolina, all located so far off the main roads that the cops never came around unless they were busting someone. Some of the bootleggers identified their homes by unusual landmarks: one house below Apex had Rock 'Em Sock 'Em Robots decking it out on the roof, still wares and tools were on the roof of another house just to keep the little ones from getting blown up, yet a third house sported purple trim. One guy's place was a country store by day, and at night the refrigerator was turned around, tapped, and beer ran directly from a keg hidden inside. I used to pick blues guitar with some older guys there at the store's back, playing until we were tired and drunk and then would go home to work in the morning. Sometimes we drank in the fields; I liked to stash beer in the toolbox on the tractor or secret a bottle of shine under the barn roof. Sometimes in the fields we'd still smell bootleggers cooking up next month's sales, as they hid out from cops and Alcoholic Beverage Control men.

Stan's paranoia intensified. Debbie, a good friend of mine from Tulsa, came for a visit, and we had a good time drinking and catching up. While she was with us, Stan went into some kind of flashback and thought I was an army prostitute or something. He started choking me with an electric cord, yelling, "I've killed whores before. With my bare hands!" I turned blue, and my legs became limber. Pulling my shotgun off the wall, Debbie coolly told Stan to back off. He let me go, and as he started calling out his social security number over and over I left with Debbie for the rest of the weekend in Raleigh. We stayed out playing pool at Five Points' Speakeasy, and it felt so great to have someone defending me.

Another time after we'd been out hustling at pool and playing cards all weekend, Stan suddenly began accusing me of looking at some man. Forcing me to drive with the lights off a good forty miles or so, he railed me the whole way. My only response was that I didn't even know who he was accusing me of looking at—which was true—and I couldn't remember looking at anyone the whole night. When we got home he choked me hard while I slept; I remember wanting to wake up but couldn't. Come morning, I woke up to fingerprint marks all over the sides of my neck and thumbprints in the center where the shirt collar dips. Not wanting to think about it, I took Quaaludes, too many Quaaludes, and slept for a long time that day and the next too. Stan was irate with me for using but denied choking me. At that time I wanted to believe in a person's sincerity so badly that I convinced myself he didn't know or remember those paranoid, violent episodes. Rationalizing made it easy to forgive and go on.

One spring, early, while the crepe myrtles in front were all budding, we moved into a different house down in Johnston County and took over some more land that had recently grown cotton. I remembered my dad's stories of picking cotton when he was a young boy and wondered if I too would have picked cotton if this field had been still committed in that way. I planted flowers all the way around the house and set out a garden so that we would feel like it was our home, not just another "croppin'" house. The house was set five miles down a dirt road with no neighbors; out back waited a pond full of loons and turtles, where I once caught what I thought was a log and was surprised to pull a turtle's head from the water literally as large as my own and to see its mate behind it looking as if they belonged at sea—we all agreed they were the largest freshwater turtles anyone had ever seen. Some of the guys wanted to shoot them, but I stood in the way, claiming they earned a right to harvest the pond since they had to be over a hundred years old.

During this time, Stan and I were shot at many times, usually escaping from a white farmer's pond. The green truck was excellent concealment, disguised in the color of the Piedmont, soon to brown, just like the leaves we cured all wet from three o'clock rains, slicing our day and slickening the roads until the rain slid off in sheets and we all chose side roads to avoid the oils rising with each speck of rain from within the fresher blacktop. Mostly we drove on crooked roads, roads amenable to Little People, twisted and bent, following the curves of streams, creeks, and rivers all across the state. Such roads were made on paths that were always Indian roads, traveled by our own ancestors after they descended into this world from the roped blanket, settled in Oconoluftee, and spread out throughout the southeast. Perhaps these roads originated when animals trailed along streams, grazing and hoofing their way along, scouted by panther, wolf, and bear. Roads still bent to follow the same watering spots and clearings, all plowed and furrowed into crops or disked into pastures now, save a few wild spaces where the trees are so thick you can still hunt and hide out without notice. They might have existed when buffalo still roamed the east before they were pushed west and killed off by the encroachers or when the great monsters in our stories stomped this earth and left ponds wherever they walked. Roads before invasion, before De Soto, before the dawn of Euroman.

Each morning Stan and I left to hunt and fish; we would pack thermoses of coffee spiked with enough whiskey to keep us warm and head for the woods without speaking. We moved stealthily through thick wooded places, where long-leaf pines shoulder willows and pop up so thick you can easily lose sight of your dog if you fall too far behind. Our world was thick with green, everything swallowed and devoured in greenness, the blanket of flora pocked by daisies. Come fall the leaves would redden and yellow, the moisture draining back into the trunk, brittling them as they fell, the branches brittling as well and tumbling down to dirt paths, blocking the way home—except for willows. The willows would simply sway in the colder breeze, retaining their own suppleness, lithe, with endurance and strength far surpassing the heavy oak branches or apple limbs. Willows stood at the mouth of every spring-fed pond or headwaters, marking the passageway between Under- and Middle worlds.

We were patient hunters, knowing what we were after and rarely coming home empty-handed. The cool air was good to breathe, and by the time you bled a kill you were filled with a healthy hunger, making the steaming organs something you couldn't refuse. It was sometimes hard to quit for the day.

It's another year, the fourth year of cropping in Willow Springs, and I am weeding again, pulling out sometimes prickly growth and finally becoming aware of my own strength. I am a "child bride" sharecropper, having gardened since early childhood, taught the environment and my place in it by my father. Side muscles are fully developed on my neck, hard-set wings follow the blades of my back and curve with each pull, and my legs are lean and taught as if I danced four days every week. I can toss around fifty-pound sacks of feed like they were boxes of oatmeal. I weigh around ninety pounds, more or less depending on the season, but am so built from working no one will chance me. If someone starts a fight while I shoot pool in town, all I have to do is let my Levi jacket off my back, exposing biceps, and the other young women back away, saying they want no trouble. It is strange for such attention to be given to my body. I am shy about my body, modest even, as is the way in my family, so I usually wear long shirts, pants, and jackets and keep myself covered.

I begin to think of working construction, though at this time women don't do that kind of work anywhere in the state. I build things all around the house and am sure I can do it. As I weed, a plan crystallizes. Come harvest, garden, sweet potato, wheat, and tobacco, when Stan leaves to do construction work in cities far away, when I usually wait on the land and take jobs within driving range, when migrant workers leave for other fields farther south, Baby No deep inside me still, I will get a job in construction.

Later that afternoon, Stan rides by on the tractor and brings me a pop and a snack. We sit in the sun admiring the growth, he complimenting me on the garden and confiding gossip about his Aunt Hazel pouring out all of his Uncle William's liquor and about William stashing a new pint in a mailbox in the back shed so she can't find it to destroy. We laugh and share time, then Stan rises to go back to a field he was considering covering in winter rye grass for the cattle. Before he leaves I call out, "You going back to construction this winter?"

"Of course. What else would I do?"

"Me too," I say and smile.

Looking at me, he starts to laugh, shakes his head, and drives away.

Soon it was fall, and we were sheeting up tobacco for auction sale in Fuquay-Varina. The hangers went back in the barns and handed down sticks covered with cured leaves, and we pulled the strings off, laying the leaves on burlap sheets, stepping the leaves down to bundle up tightly, and then carrying them away to market for auction. Once at the tobacco houses the bundles would be categorized and priced according to quality. Auctioneers with their steady vocal drumming would hawk the bundles to the industry and away from the fields. We always brought top dollar on the bulk of our crop and stayed around the next couple of days for the sales. Afterward we'd get together with other fieldworkers and barbecue a hog (usually farm rustled, sometimes actually wild boars) on an open pit. The preferred sauce was vinegar and red pepper, with the pepper outweighing the vinegar by a good deal of heat. Someone else always killed them, but sometimes I'd get stuck gutting the hogs because everybody hated the task. A few women would begin to prepare the chitlins while a couple of men would singe off the wirelike hog hair. We'd sit right by the pit, brushing on the sauce until the tenderloins got ready. After sneaking away with most of that delicacy, I'd let someone else take over. Music would blast through the empty fields over a PA with guys playing everything from Brownie McGhee to Hendrix till way past three o'clock in the morning.

I took my share of the crop money and put it away except for some money to pay a watch repairman to fix my dad's old railroad pocket watch I'd broken as a child. There was a watchmaker in Angier at that time who was pretty amazing with watches, so I took the gold watch without my dad knowing about it and had him repair it. When done, I gave the watch back to my dad, apologizing for breaking it years before. He still has that watch to this day.

We settled in at home, covering the stubbled lands with winter crops and moving cattle down to feed. Stan and I settled in to fish, hunt, and put up meat, sometimes drying strips in the kitchen on tobacco sticks and mostly filling the freezer on the back porch. I'd spend a good part of the day pulling clothes through the wringer washer, quilting, or making cornhusk dolls from the corn crop down behind the house. Sometimes I'd sit outside and write blues songs or paint, use the Nikkormat FT2 camera I got while working nights in a drugstore, weave, make pottery, or sometimes I'd just be. It seemed easy to settle without a feeling of falling behind.

There was an opening for someone to break horses (along with a room and management possibilities) for an RCA cowboy named Jimmy Ray Pleasant over near Garner. Having worked horses all my life, I thought it would be good to have a steady income from something I knew well. Jimmy had lost a kidney riding broncs but couldn't give up horses. He teased me about my size and asked if I could lift a saddle onto a horse seventeen hands high. Riding across his land, we talked horses for most of a morning; afterward, he tested me on lunge lines and green-broke horses before bringing over a little Arabian filly, nervous, shy, and never saddled. Living with too much violence, I was familiar with such shyness, a certain spookiness that comes on one side when something moves too fast. It was pure joy to keep up while she gave me all she had, as I sized her efforts to get rid of me before she made them. Bringing me a Colt 45 tallboy, Jimmy showed me my new room, which I stayed in half of the week. I was given complete reign of the place and the livestock as well as say-so over the hired wranglers, since Jimmy drove a gas truck and stayed on the road a lot and Lee Ann, his wife, a veterinarian, wasn't home much either.

I was happy, finally back with horses and still my own boss most of the week. Jimmy brought me a beautiful buckskin named Kansas, seventeen hands high, whom no one but he could ride until I saddled him up. I used Kansas to run in the horses and check fence.

The men wranglers brought in mustangs from roundups and bred horses from all over the country. I'd get fresh horse scent on myself from the trailers as soon as they came in. When no one was looking I would sneak the horses licorice root and sing to them like children while throwing hay and watering them. I also tied their hair through my cuff buttonholes or belt loops, a childhood trick designed to hasten familiarity.

If mean young studs threw the wranglers, Jimmy would call me over to prove myself (I'd comply, always insisting though on my extra fee of a case of beer, carton of smokes, or bottle of whiskey for doing their work). Jimmy took a personal delight in my outriding the men. Sometimes the broncs threw me too, and I'd get so mad I'd slap them up or give them a punch right on the nose. If a horse reared straight back when he bucked, it would really make me angry—not only was no horse going to boss me, but they could kill themselves doing that. I'd get back up after being thrown, gradually earning respect from the men.

Come cold weather, just after Stan left for Greenville with his winter job crew, there were fewer horses to break, and I had time to pursue my other work goal in construction. A friend of a Pleasant wrangler talked me into applying up at Inland. The Inland boss laughed me off until I took off my jacket, showing just enough muscle to convince him. He then handed me some papers to sign, admitting that to hire a woman, a blondie breed at that, would boost their statistics quota and help with bidding contracts. I began as a carpenter's helper and as a laborer wrecking concrete forms, soon driving nails and spikes as straight as journeymen. I moved into heavy equipment soon thereafter. Some guys at first had a hard time with a woman on the site and one time switched my sixty-pound power tamp for one weighing over a hundred. The unexpected weight threw me all over the ground before I could let loose and tore my rib away from my breastbone. I didn't tell anyone about the exchange, and the crew became my ardent defender thereafter.

Stan found it difficult to accept my working construction. Breaking horses was bad enough, but now I was working in towns around men he didn't know, and he grew jealous. I never did step out on him or anything like that, though I had ample opportunity, and the more he accused me, the more I considered it. My dad, however, didn't raise me that way; if I was going to cheat on Stan I would have given him the dignity of leaving first. Stan began to treat me like I was being unfaithful and started cuffing me when he would return, making clear that he wanted me home on the land while he was away and it was my place to be there. The more he insisted, the more I stayed with the horses. I wasn't trying to make trouble, but I didn't like being accused without any wrongdoing on my part.

We went on this way until one weekend when he came home, brought me some food, and I got deathly ill. His reaction was odd—Stan stayed right by my side the entire time I was sick, looking guilty. I began to wonder if he'd poisoned me but put it out of my head quickly. Those kinds of thoughts aren't good for the heart, I reasoned.

Interestingly, while his suspicion and paranoia grew, we began to talk on the phone a great deal while he was away. We'd never had a phone before, never thought of having one until I had gotten ill. One night we spoke on the phone during a Fraizer boxing match, talking in between rounds and commenting on the fight during them. The line went dead halfway through the fight; a few hours later I tried to call Stan back. When I asked for my husband's room, the hotel manager covered the phone, but I could still hear his exclamation, "That guy has a *wife* on the phone. He's married!" I couldn't imagine any reason a hotel manager might have cared, except that there were adultery laws in North Carolina at that time, so I concluded that something was afoot. A while later my insurance man sent me a bill listing a new white Trans Am under an unknown woman's name. When I called to ask about the change, he said, "Your husband told me to add it to his policy. I must have put it on yours by mistake."

Another spring had arrived. I waited for Stan to return home for a weekend. As soon as he arrived, I asked him to take me out to dinner to celebrate our setting-up-house anniversary. He complained he was too tired to go anywhere; I asked if he wanted just to go to bed early, and he offered the same excuse and then asked me to fix him a meal. Figuring he definitely had someone else by then, I decided not to fight or give him more reason to lie about it. I announced, "I guess you are too tired for me. I'm leaving," picked up a small bag I'd already packed, and walked out the door. I turned around once, told him to have a good life, loaded my animals, and drove away.

By my twentieth birthday in 1978, I rented my own place, a tarpaper shack adorned with cardboard windows. The floors were so crooked and warped that a marble dropped on one end of the house might travel through each one of the three rooms before stopping. People said the shack looked like a drunk built it. The floor was so rotted it would break loose if you stepped too hard. There was no running water, pitcher pump, or bathroom, so I dug an outhouse off the back side and filled it with lime to work as a decomposing agent. I didn't mind having no running water; it seemed a blessing, an escape from early memories. I owned no furniture except for what I built at the shop on the Inland construction job, but a cooler did serve as a refrigerator, and an old ice box painted bright orange kept meat. A bat used to hang on the front porch edge by day and fly off into the night in search of insects. Once I came home late from night classes and the bat seemed so still I couldn't believe it would fly again. It didn't. Come morning it was still hanging upside down on the edge, wings wrapped tightly around its little body like a shroud, dead.

My brother was attempting to get a GED at Wake Tech, where I'd gotten mine only a few years before. Unemployed, he was using drugs and drinking and wasn't moving forward. He was still beating my mother and taking her money for his habits, so I offered him an alternative—stay with me and go to classes. During this time the Rolling Stones were making a national tour, and Etta James and Rod Stewart were opening. The Kiowa guitar wizard Jesse Ed Davis played with Stewart, making us proud. I headed out to Greensboro and left my brother in charge of the house. He had sealed off the cardboard windows with duct tape due to the cold. Just as he was getting out a bedroll to sleep on, he smelled gas fumes, traceable to some tubing coming through a split in the floor that in turn led to a gas tank, which had a valve slightly open. Much later my brother and I moved out of the shack because we had no heat and winter was hard that year.

I ran into Stan's oldest sister, Wanda, at a store. She told me William, the old man from the tobacco fields, had burned alive in his Falcon. He had been too drunk to drive, hit a tree, and the car burst into flames with him in it. I missed him immediately. I was drinking already, but with this news I increased my limit steadily. I hid it well, but mornings sometimes shook so much I could barely dress myself. By the time I was on the job I'd taken something to break the shakes, even if it was shaving lotion.

I kept both of my jobs until I was arrested for drunkenness and ended up in detox. The first thing I did in the hospital was to tell Stan I would never come home. I would be the first in my entire lineage to leave a marriage, and it troubled me. I asked for nothing but my freedom.

My mother was in the psychiatric wing of the same hospital where I dried out. Though I knew it was possible she wouldn't recognize or remember me, I thought of visiting her but was never allowed off the detox floor. I was allowed only to pass by and visit with catatonic and comatose youngsters whom no one wanted at home.

One such boy sat in a wheelchair in the hall all day. A nurse would push him out in the morning and wheel him back at night. He was maybe seven years younger than me, Black, and stared like the walls didn't exist, like he could see clear to the mountains and wasn't letting go of the vision. He was the only person I talked to there, and I spoke to him every day and hoped somewhere inside that he knew. I wanted to take him away, give him hope, and tell him he could look around and find something else to cling to, a person, another place, a life. One day he cried while I spoke; the nurses said it was only a reflex, but I knew he was in there. I could feel it but didn't know how to get through. Talking to him made me realize I was in my own prison too.

When I left detox I was too shamed out to return to my regular jobs, so I picked up odd jobs here and there. I discovered that my brother was skipping his Wake Tech classes and hitchhiking hours away over to my dad's house, where he'd get checks from my mom, party up, and scoot back to our place by evening. Shortly after, my brother simply gave up school and moved into my dad's house again. When I would stop by, he was always smoking up and lying around terrorizing my chronically mentally ill mother.

I told my brother that he should get a job, and he said he would if he knew how. He was my little brother — no matter what he'd done to me I cared and felt responsible for him. So I took him over to a construction outfit in Raleigh, helped him put in an application, and accompanied him to the back office to interview. He was strong from working out with weights, which I think he'd begun way back in reform school, and from fixing dented car bodies in the driveway. I pointed out his strength and youth and said he'd be good at heavy equipment operation. My brother was hired and learned quickly.

When I was satisfied that my brother would soon be on his own and maybe carve a life out for himself away from my parents, I decided to hit the road again. I spent some time moving in and out of places and tried working in an office, coding insurance for computer entry for Farmer's Insurance. One of my coworkers was the wife of a PLO member, and she was being hounded by the feds to work as an informer and was very afraid. I was also leery of office people. Working inside wasn't for me. I couldn't understand office politics and women who spent more time in front of a mirror and chatting than working. They seemed superficial and not bright; working with them reminded me of watching bad television. Once the guys from the Inland construction company were building a restaurant across the street, so I began spending my lunch breaks with them. The women in my office had fits over it, complaining to our boss that I came back to work after lunch smelling like sawdust.

I would run into Stan on occasion, or he would stop by, still trying to find out why I left and why I wouldn't come home. Still under thirty, his hair had turned gray. Once when I asked what happened to him, he pointed at me and said, "I thought you were coming back."

"I told you I was leaving," I answered, confused.

He had the strangest look in his eyes, a look like a puppy gives you when you've scolded him for chewing something up. "I didn't know you were serious," he admitted. "I thought you were just saying things."

I walked away, wondering why anyone would say they were leaving someone if they had no intention of going away. It seemed bizarre that he didn't take me seriously when we'd spent all those years together. I thought by now he'd know something about me.

Apparently not.

I never did explain myself to him. I didn't talk much about my feelings and needs, since such openness often proved dangerous. People might gather such information to use against you, to find vulnerable areas of attack or emotional control, or to gossip and enlarge hardship details. So I never truly understood the point of sharing emotionally back then. I only learned to divulge my hardcore deeds, which prevented people from knowing I had the gentle soul I had, scaring them away from getting too close and keeping enough distance to prevent violation of the body and soul.

I decided to go to the ocean, a place where I knew no one and where I could still fish and hopefully find work—getting away from everything, trying to get the 'bacca out of my system and replace it with fish and oysters. To run again.

Before I left, I met with Stan again, more out of guilt for seeing my ex turn gray than anything else. Believing time has a healing property useful in processing and understanding the fullness of purposeful living, I had promised myself to sever all contact with him for at least one year before considering further conversation. He had been on his own for more than that time now, and I thought maybe he'd had time to reflect and would perhaps want to work things out. I began by saying I didn't want to talk about anything that happened before and that if he could abide by that and just start over I would be willing to reconsider reconciliation.

Looking paranoid and constantly looking around, Stan admitted he was seeing someone. He went on to claim that if I came back I'd probably just leave him again. This someone was a white city girl he had met at a pool hall in Raleigh. She got hold of me a few days later, complaining openly about his wishes to have her work with him in the fields, wondering if I had done that when I was with him and asking how to deal with his posttraumatic episodes and violence. I pitied her, knowing it would never last.

Later, I heard that before she left Stan the city girl had two babies and abandoned them there on the lands. Stan then visited my dad, looking for me and confiding that he was mistaken to have lost me and would never find someone as dedicated and hard-working as me again.

Time had passed, though, and I was used to living on my own. Though I felt sorry for Stan and knew in my heart I could have returned and made the marriage work, it was none of my business anymore.

The great God of Nature has placed us in different situations. It is true that he has endowed you with many superior advantages; but he has not created us to be your slaves. We are a separate people! He has given each their lands, under distinct considerations and circumstances; he has stocked yours with cows, ours with buffalo; yours with hog, ours with bear; yours with sheep, ours with deer. He has, indeed, given you an advantage in this, that your cattle are tame and domestic while ours are wild and demand not only a larger space for range, but art to hunt and kill them; they are, nevertheless, as much our property as other animals are yours, and ought not to be taken away without our consent, or for something equivalent.

Corn Tassel, Cherokee, July 1785

When I was a boy I saw the white man far off and was told that he was my enemy. I could not shoot him as I would a wolf or a bear, yet he came upon me. My horse and fields he took from me. He said he was my friend— He gave me his hand in friendship; I took it, he had a snake in the other; his tongue was forked; he lied and he stung me. I asked for but a small piece of this land, enough to plant and live on far to the south— a spot where I could place the ashes of my kindred— a place where my wife and child could live. This was not granted me. I am about to leave Florida forever and have done nothing to disgrace it. It was my home; I loved it, and to leave it is like burying my wife and child. I have thrown away my rifle and have taken the hand of the white man, and now I say take care of me!

Coacoochee (Wild Cat), Seminole,
upon his surrender to the U.S. Army, 1858

Doublehead, indisputably a brave Cherokee warrior, once fought the enemy so often and so well that he began to take on the traits of this enemy's people, implementing practices that were against the people's natural ways, and in doing so endangered his own. Some of these practices involved disrespecting the women's decisions on treatment of captives, cannibalism, and the killing of enemy children. He was executed to ensure that the ways of his own people would survive.

6

Oceans, Rivers

The Carolina coast seemed foreign in 1979, although my sister and I had spent a weekend there years before, and I had surf-cast once off tobacco season. The land meeting the sea bore a certain unfamiliar strangeness. Having known only plains and woodlands, I believed oceans held mystery dissimilar enough to afford change, to reorchestrate fluidity in the tides and swells of my own path.

With no previous experience, I took a part-time job as a night auditor at Captain's Inn Resort Motel, supplemented with a bartending position at the Sandbar Lounge. I was looking to clear enough pay for rent and still have free hours for a new life of fishing and long peaceful walks with my dogs on the sands of the Outer Banks of North Carolina.

A spacious flat a block off the beach was available for $120 per month. The ocean view filled the front window on the top floor of the three-story wood-frame building barely holding its own in the coastal breeze. On a clear day you could see out across sand dunes topped with sea oats and white-capped blue-green waters forever lapping a plains-flat shore. Come storms, the house would sway. A hurricane hovering off the coast, I would throw a yellow slicker on and stand on the front porch, where the force of the wind would momentarily suspend me above the wooden boards before I took leave of the building to seek more stable ground.

I learned to lock my knees to fish all night from the piers, waking only for a pull on the line and only long enough to pull in the catch before casting again and sleeping. Come morning, the sky crimsoned and yellowed above the eerie waters; the eeriness presented itself through creatures, which by appearance should have been fossils yet still swam and took bloodworm bait, creatures that proved the ocean is no place to pleasure swim but you did anyway, sometimes coming out with blood letting from your bare feet into the sand, spreading and absorbing a foot or so around where you stood, blood letting from the bite of something you might never see even if you had stepped directly into its mouth or back fin.

Soon, much of the motion of drawing fish from water welled in me. Once I was casting off a jetty, the blues were running and it was hot, and I snagged one who simply turned his head and bit the line, breaking free. Without hesitation, I leapt from the rocks and dove into the water, catching the blue with my bare hands, holding it above the break, and tossing it up near my rod. When I couldn't climb out from where I'd jumped into the treacherous waters, nearby fishermen — smiling at my refusal to let the fish go — threw me a nylon rope to draw myself from the ocean.

I love the water. A sea turtle wanders by, looking as if it were blind, its eyes cast glassy gray. I am happy it has so much freedom here, though, knowing of tourists who steal their eggs and poachers who drag them away whenever they can, I pity him.

Ducks dive as pelicans swoop from the skies, both piercing water for fish and sometimes for shellfish, which the gulls drop from the blue onto gray and black jetties before devouring white meat and clear gel. Some say gulls can see a piece of food from two miles away. Standing in the surf, I throw crackers in the air, and they strike down to eat while still in flight, floating on air just in front of me until so many wings extend and curl, so many beaks open and close that I feel they could lift and pin me like laundry on a line if they so decided. Returning to my rod, I fish with them.

For months I stayed alone fishing, swimming, working long nights to enjoy days to myself, watching the dogs chase the edging tide all along the island coast. Inevitably, however, I returned to a liquid more dominating than the ocean. Far away now from the fields, from lands providing me with purpose, my mentality lapsed into the insensibility of more hardcore life. I began hanging out after my shift was long behind, hustling pool, holding fast to the bottles and cans that lured me surer than bloodworms do flounder.

Drinking puts you in places you should never be, with people you have no business with, and calls it love. A guy with long dark hair and deep brown eyes who came in near closing took only one look at me before kissing me fully on the mouth, then lifted me completely off my feet. I went out with that guy that first night and the next three following, then he moved in, taking over my place and my life before I blinked myself awake.

Tom was descended from traditional Native families on both sides but raised in Charlotte in gangs. His dad was a union truck driver and a hard-working man. Though there was no amount of effort I didn't make to flash Tom back into the other side of being Indian—taking him to the rez to camp, to gatherings to remind him where his own ancestors came from in better days—it never took hold. To him he was a warrior, to me a mixed-up mixed-blood street warrior. My dad's version of a warrior was a defender of the people with otter pelt–covered arms. Tom's world, in contrast, consisted of street fighting, stabbing, drive-by shooting, jail, prison, parole, and throwing up on his own feet in the late-night street—violence. Violence I knew, having been surrounded by it all my life. At the time he was on parole for hired arson, having gained release by participating in a program that concealed identity but revealed details of how criminals succeed in crimes.

I fell into his troubled world as certain as he centered himself in mine. We both drank daily, and with each day Tom showed me he was someone I could never reason with. His emotions almost always manifested as anger—waking up suspicious of me, he would hold a gun to my head while he thought I slept, clicking it without knowing which chamber was loaded. We both slept fully clothed, he with his boots on, as if every moment harbored danger.

My life with Tom didn't seem unusual at the time. I'd spent much of my youth surviving, so I was used to holding my guard up and hanging tough. Looking back, I believed I deserved to be treated badly. I was a failure after all, the bad, bad girl my mother rejected, the one who needed correcting, the first one in the family to ever leave a relationship. I typically remained quiet and still while he endangered me, though sometimes I laughed aloud at the intimidation, tempting my own certainty to survive. I wasn't afraid of death, so there was little he could do that would make me openly react.

We got news at that time that my grandma in Canada, my mother's
mother, had died of a bad heart. I went down to the water and prayed
for her, hoping she would cross over to a good place where Europeans
might go when they leave here. I prayed for my mother to weather it
well. I prayed for my grandpa, who would be on his own now. I was
sad but at the same time felt a strange sense of relief and anger. One
less person could hurt me now.

Undoubtedly because of my relationship with Tom, I became increasingly mean during this time of my life, drinking, fighting, and getting in trouble. Since childhood, I had fought and defended those
in trouble, and drinking exaggerated that impulse. I wasn't afraid of
anything when tuned up.

Once Tom and I spotted two beach-bum rednecks picking on a
Lumbee man called Jabbo. Even though some Cherokee people claim
mixed feelings about the Lumbees, my family remembered them because of their taking masks from the KKK in earlier years, so I leapt to
Jabbo's defense; Tom joined me, not fighting for anything ethically,
just wanting to damage things. Outnumbered, the rednecks quickly
jumped into a Trans Am, but Tom jumped onto the hood of their car,
kicking out the windshield and hood scoop with his boot. Grabbing
tightly the collar of the biggest guy and trying to pull him out of the
car to finish what he'd started, I ripped the shirt clean off of his body,
leaving only the sleeves behind.

I was still drunk and even fought the cops as they took me in because I found disrespectful their pointing fingers at us. They had to
handcuff me several times because I kept slipping off the cuffs and
throwing them back. Tom was taken in for property damage, while
they charged me with putting the rednecks in fear of their lives and
assault with intent. My charges were later dismissed in court because
both rednecks stood over six feet tall and each weighed over two hundred pounds. Tom was ordered to pay for the car's damage, but he
never did, and nothing ever came of it.

Another time when playing pool and circulating the tip jar for a
fellow barkeep, I was called a bitch for asking for money by a jarhead,
a marine. Tom's brother, Jeff, who was watching everything from the
door, came in to defend me. A fight broke out, stools and chairs were

tossed, and pool cues were broken. The fight swelled to a brawl, until the entire clientele was up in arms.

During the melee, the jarhead got my defender down on the concrete and pulled a blade. Instinctively wanting to get the marine off of Jeff no matter what happened to me, I lunged at him and jerked him up by his camouflage jacket. Turning and facing me, he slit at my stomach with the knife. I feigned unconsciousness long enough for Jeff to recover, and then he beat the shit out of that guy. Another marine grabbed me hard up from the ground, putting a blade at my cheek until I reached my fingers in and around his right eye. It loosened, and he started screaming. I felt guilty about that eye for years afterward, even though the guy meant to kill me. Dislodging the eyeball affected me so profoundly I have never been able to fight well physically since.

The fear of my own strength was suddenly upon me.

The one time I got into serious trouble was when my only crime was bumping into a preacher's car in the parking lot of a Newport gas station. It was a tiny dent, and the preacher himself didn't even care. Suddenly, about twelve redneck-looking guys who were having a pit barbecue picnic nearby began running toward me. I ran, not knowing what else to do and not being protected by my man. Dashing into a large junkyard adjacent to the gas station, I hid underneath an old Buick.

A snake appeared next to my face, startling me. I made a childish sound, and suddenly arms reached in for me. I was pulled and dragged out from my hiding place, fighting all the way. As the barbecue picnickers started reading me my rights, I realized they were off-duty cops (actually, as I found out later, highway patrolmen). They took me out in the country, handcuffing, ankle cuffing, thumb cuffing, and working me over before driving across the county to the Beaufort jail. Seeing how mangled I was, the Beaufort cops refused to let the off-duty cops drive off with me unaccompanied. I thanked them for following us in and asked the jailer (who knew me) for some medical attention.

Because the Beaufort jail contained no facilities for women, oftentimes I and other women stayed in the drunk tank even if we weren't inebriated and regardless of the length of confinement. The drunk tank was made of concrete and steel bars, with no air conditioning (unlike the men's cells). I heard that was the same jail where Jo Ann Little in self-defense had recently ice-picked a molesting guard to death and fled to New York for amnesty. Maybe she killed him in this same cell.

I became friends with a Black woman imprisoned for murdering her husband. She claimed he fell on shattered glass that pierced his heart, but almost everyone inside claimed innocence, so I never really knew the truth but expressed compassion nonetheless. Because she was in for a long haul, my friend could get smokes, Kool cigarettes that made you feel like you were in fresh air no matter where you were locked up. She also could get candy and cards, and we played spades all night long, not caring about the time. I enjoyed her company.

I had little patience in jail and didn't tolerate bragging or chatter that interrupted our card games. Sometimes young white girls would be brought in on drunken-in-public or runaway charges. They'd strut around bragging about how bad they were, until I'd look over at the long-time woman and ask, "Your turn or mine?" I'd jump up, take the dinner tray out of the girl's hands, flex up my biceps, and tell them to wish to get out before night comes. Usually that's all it took. Scared, they'd start crying to the guard to get someone to bail them out.

Generally, I was safer inside the jail than out because Tom beat me. The first punch comes unexpectedly and knocks me completely senseless, my arms numb and dangling, then rabbit punches are fired into my face, rocking my head like a punching bag actually hard enough to herniate my vertebrae and retina.

"STUPID BITCH! STUPID, STUPID BITCH!" he screams as he beats me. "I'LL KILL YOU! YOU STUPID BITCH! NO ONE COULD EVER LOVE YOU! YOU LIKE THIS, DON'T YOU!"

On and on through the entire ordeal. He might as well be screaming to the Buggers that torture my mother, the way his voice takes on her mental expression in tone, rage, and immediacy.

Always, upon waking, Tom would claim no memory of anything and ask me what happened. Given my mother's shock amnesia, sometimes I believed him. It was easy. She had no recollection of our childhood and often fabricated one to make it easier for her to deal with her loss. Blackouts I understood—they were tangible and provided a vehicle for immediate forgiveness, for emotional denial. Lack of memory made it easy for me to deny my own needs and to focus on his, nearly reversing responsibility and switching roles. Often while cuffing me, Tom would ask why I "let" him do that to me, protesting that he was no good for me yet in practically the same breath admitting he'd stalk and kill me if I ever tried to leave him.

He was a jealous man. Once when my teeth were knocked out he refused to allow replacement dentures for six months because he imagined I only wanted teeth to attract attention. I literally couldn't raise my eyes without him accusing me of coming on to someone. He said he'd kill me so often that I got used to hearing it. But I also knew he wasn't exaggerating. He meant it.

He made sure that I always sported bruises, cuts, or breaks somewhere on my body before we went out in public. Sometimes my eyes were swollen from the upper lid clear down to my cheek bottoms, my nose laid over and cut, my lips ripped and oozing. Proving that he never meant to hurt me sometimes meant a trip to the emergency room, though Tom would tell the medical staff that I'd been in a wreck or attacked by a stranger. They would respond with cervical collars, stitches, and bandages and then would unwittingly send me home for more.

I never reported him because of my dislike for police and assumption that their intervention would complicate rather than fix things anyway. Women's shelters were something I never heard of until over a decade later.

I drank to survive Tom. How could I possibly have taken the abuse sober?

We were getting arrested so often that we decided to move off the island and into a trailer just on the edge of the mainland. I had been drinking so much with him that I'd sold everything I owned (which truthfully wasn't much); when not working, I bummed change to drink more.

In that trailer, far off of main roads and fully surrounded by woods, I began to separate myself from Tom mentally and started standing up to him because he spent a lot of time on the islands without me. One night he was home drinking and stole my truck, leaving me at the trailer with no wheels. I was drunk too, and later that night something snapped in me, just taking over completely, and I could feel myself getting angrier and angrier. I took Tom's ax handle cured in motor oil to strengthen the wood and hitchhiked to the beaches looking for him and my truck.

When I came down the strip, wearing a stained leather jacket and clutching the club, his brothers and friends were gathered in a parking lot. They saw me and parted with nods and curiosity, literally stepping backward and making a space for me to confront him. Although they were all men and were his friends or brothers, most didn't like the way he treated me and rarely defended him (sometimes some offered to distract him for awhile so I could escape, though they never took action when I agreed).

Stalking by them, I spied Tom, standing with his arms wrapped around some white biker chick, drunker than hell, so drunk he didn't see me. Reaching over and grabbing his long hair, I brandished the club and ordered him to throw down my keys. The biker momma started crying the blues, claiming she didn't know he was mine. Glancing up, I said I had no quarrel with her and she could have him if she wanted—after I was done. He started cussing but was too drunk to defend himself with his hair pulled that way. I started swinging the club, thinking I should lay him out like he had me so many times, intending to leave him now and leave him wounded on the street without mercy, not caring if he caught up to me later and did kill me.

Just then I was shoved from behind into the parking lot chain-link fence, a barrel hard against my head. A cop whispered, "Move and I'll blow your brains out, Bitch."

The police handcuffed and threw me into their car, but I was drunk and worked my way out of the cuffs. Throwing them out the window, I demanded, "GET MY FUCKING TRUCK KEYS FROM HIM!" Hitting the car with a club and cussing more before cuffing me again, the police did get my keys from Tom and had him sign charges against me before taking me to holding. Tom's dad showed up, pissed, and informed the cops that though this man beat me every day, they had done nothing about it, but the first time I'd turned the tables they had thrown me in. He told them, "He may be my son, but she should have killed the bastard." When Tom's dad threatened to sue the police, they let me go.

I turned legal aged, and, though I became determined to take my life back, matters became worse. After I was released, Tom didn't come home for awhile, which was fine with me. Late one night, he did show up, tuned up and really plastered as usual.

Playing solitaire, I refused to take him for more wine—more red wine, more rot gut, just one more jug of Richard's Wild Irish Rose. Soon I was driving my truck with steel against my side and fresh blood trickling from my nose and ear. It was raining hard, I wanted to brake, and he was pissed, ranting about the song on the radio—I think it was "Blue Skies"—and ordering me to turn the music down.

I tried to talk, to put the right words together, to get my message across, to tell him I wanted out—out of the drunkenness, out of the truck, out of the "relationship," out of everything.

"It's not good here," I carefully said. "I don't think it should go further. I think it's time . . ."

"Turn off that damn radio," he said.

"Just hear me out."

"You're leaving *ME*? No FUCKING way! I'LL KILL BOTH of us!" Flooring my foot onto the gas pedal, Tom grabbed the wheel, sending the truck careening into a road sign and then off a cliffed embankment.

Limitless air. I flung my arm across his chest in some instinctual motion to prevent him from hitting the windshield. The force of the act sent him out the back windshield, and the truck began flipping over and over, side over side and end over end. Having been thrown into the bed of the pickup, my back banged the metal box each time it overturned.

And then it was raining and raining, and I couldn't move even a finger. I was lying on my back in mud with rainwater creeping up my face and the truck's headlights staring from fifty or so feet away. The water was just below my nostrils, and I would soon drown in the wet, wet dark. For what seemed like hours—though I have no idea how much time actually passed—I believed this was my last view of earth since the water was steadily rising. I felt a lifting and I was free. Despite my predicament, the elation of freedom filled me with joy.

Eventually, a man's voice called out of the darkness above, asking if anyone was down where I lay. I yelled back, and he found me just as the waters almost smothered my breathing. I was carried up the embankment and onto the shoulder of the highway. My rescuer was a biker, in the classic sense of the word—a white Hell's Angel in black leather on a Harley, a fugitive who promised to contact authorities even though he couldn't stay around himself. Standing on the side of the road in the night rain, I watched his bike pull away. I lived still, and I stiffened rather than relaxed at this realization.

A Black marine stopped on his way to Cherry Point and called in on a radio for help, and the state patrol and sheriff arrived about the same time. I couldn't feel anything damaged, though I experienced some problems with balance. They found Tom unconscious on the roadside, and I was "allowed" to accompany him in the ambulance to the hospital.

Upon arriving at the emergency room, they took him in on a stretcher and left me in the waiting room, since he had told the doctors he had sustained brain damage from the impact and was dying. Tom's family began to arrive. After about an hour, the doctors reported that he was fine and only required two stitches.

By this time I noticed my teeth were coming free from their sockets and that I was swallowing blood. I asked the triage nurse if they could check me out and mentioned feeling woozy. My x-rays and urinalysis were run while they finished sewing up Tom's head. After those tests, I got dressed and joined his family in the waiting room. He came out, his family making a big fuss and offering to take him to his mother's for recovery. Simultaneously, a stretcher was wheeled in, and some nurses asked me if I needed help to lay on it. I laughed at first, thinking they were teasing—without losing consciousness, I doubted I could be seriously hurt. The nurses calmly read the report about my multiple injuries and told me I was bleeding to death internally. About the time they put the iv in my arm, I began to feel pain and realized the seriousness of my condition.

I was hospitalized for an extensive stay but never had one visitor (Tom never informed my family, I later learned), and parts of me never completely recovered. It was over a year before I could eat solid food.

That ridiculous "accident" cost me my truck, my health, my physical strength, everything. The truck was mangled, twisted, and totaled, and the insurance policy had lapsed. The last payment had been made only three months before, but my insurance bill had accidentally been sent to my former address in Willow Springs and never forwarded. For quite some time, I took steps only with the aid of a walker. The doctor refused to sign my work disability papers until I had the ability to pay him, which never happened because I couldn't draw disability without a doctor's notice. Stupid man. I did collect unemployment on my old job due to wrongful termination for letting me go when I was in the hospital.

I was told that I would never be able to work sustained manual labor again. What a difficult turn of events to accept. Other than a few odd jobs, manual labor was all I knew, and I couldn't fathom not being able to function physically on that level. Not being able to lift a paperback book or eat easily, my extremities blackened from subsurface bleeding, and my breathing laborious, I felt useless. Despite my post-birthday resolution, I'd been conquered.

When my release date came, Tom showed up in a beat-up Datsun, declaring I was going with him, like it or not. Standing, holding onto my walker, I begged him to leave me there, protesting that I wanted out of the relationship. I had had enough.

He was pretty creative when he wanted something. Knowing I was happier in the mountains, Tom took me to Cherokee almost straight from the hospital. It was snowing lightly. We visited some relatives on the way, but I wasn't of mind to have him meet my parents, even though we passed within a mile of their place, so we pitched camp in the woods just before the flakes accumulated. Within three days we were snowed in completely. It was a dry snow, the kind that blankets the ground and still blows freely in the air, the kind in which a Coleman lamp provides just enough heat in a tent covered three feet under.

I became pregnant within the time it took the river to partially freeze, by a man I didn't want to be with, a man who claimed countless times he was sterile. I knew it immediately, and I also was aware that I carried a boy. The only thing positive was that this baby was conceived on Tsa la gi soil, the parents were both of the same people, and I had been sober since the night of the wreck, so there was little danger of the baby being FAS.

I went down into town alone, under the guise of washing clothes at the Laundromat, while Tom stayed at camp cutting ice to fish. I got hold of a cousin, and after we prayed together I finished washing clothes and made it back to our camp just after Tom had fallen asleep. I sat by the fire, still burning hard, and wondered what I was doing with him and how long I could endure.

We returned to the coast, mostly because his parents were living there and he knew we could make a living harvesting the waters with their boats. We rented a century-and-a-half-old, two-story clapboard house for $150 a month outside Newport, North Carolina. The living room on the northern corner was the original house, shaped by low ceilings and flat-board walls. A kettle could just be squeezed in and hung inside the fireplace. The rest of the house had been built around that room as the inhabitant's family had grown. Just off the living room to the west was a room that I worked to make into a nursery. Our bedroom was just south of the living room, and the kitchen was on the south side. At the farthest end away from the kitchen door was another addition: the only bathroom. It was fairly modern, but being away from any heat source the pipes would freeze up in the winter. Upstairs there were two rooms, in which I set up my sewing materials in one and my guitars, photography, and art supplies in the other. The house was completely skirted with porches, which were covered with a tin roof. On the front of the house a wraparound porch sat upon a stone foundation. Tom would sell there loads of junk and antiques he obsessively collected under the guise of yard sales—old iron-tread Singers, clear-glass milk bottles, colored-glass electrical caps, and whatever else we dragged out of the woods and refinished for sale. It appeared easier for him to give attention and be compassionate to inanimate objects.

Our landlords, descendants of the house's builders, lived next door to the south. There were no other neighbors for miles except a house across the road in which, according to the landlords, the tenant accidentally scalded her baby to death in a bathtub a few years before. The landlords also claimed, "Things happened in the house you're living in too." They never let on what "things" exactly occurred, just that there had been some "mean family fights in there."

Indeed, there was something peculiar about our new house. One moment it felt lively and safe, and the next, danger seemed imminent to me. It seemed haunted, and every time I was alone there that feeling grew stronger. Though such solitude should have been peaceful for me, it became a time of uneasiness.

Outside, I could work all day around the house without the slightest trace of queer feelings. The sun was hot and the air fresh, but inside it was always just slightly too cool, even in July. Out back there was acreage clear to the tree line, so I requested and received permission to put in a garden. I don't think the landlords realized I was from sharecropping and meant a full garden, but that's what I put in, around a half-acre, and full of everything I loved to grow and eat. I spent all my time tending this garden, turning loose the hunting dogs and sheltie. When loosened, they would bound through the rows and sit by my side as I weeded and tended the greens.

Working dirt there, I began to feel rooted again, but Tom's deeper problems began to surface more. Soon I pretended to be asleep when he'd come home (every second or third night)—if I was sleeping he'd only slap, but if awake I'd be beaten, beaten while being accused of snagging out on him, or using him, or committing some other crime, all accusations never grounded in fact or true. I was punished regardless, much the same as when I was a child and my mother would conform her discipline to her delusions rather than our actions.

Now that I was pregnant for him, Tom suddenly started to bring me flowers, almost always red roses and almost always preceding or following a beating. Those flowers symbolized for me the love-hate relationship he had for me, his woman, his enemy. The flowered beatings became a symbol of the pattern of alcohol, a Wild Irish Rose, the truer enemy. Abstaining from alcohol for months and months, it became clear to me that we had no tolerance and protection from its monotonous waving motion.

We did work together at the sea, though I wasn't as useful as before the "accident." I did my best. I had to. Mostly Tom and I hauled nets from a skiff, filled with jumping mullet. We also oystered, clammed, gathered scallop, and fished from piers and from the surf. Sometimes we'd stay out in the waters of the sound and sea for days, and sometimes we'd just go a portion of the day. There were fish houses all along the sound where we sold our catch, and for the tourist trade we harvested sand dollars, brown and fuzzy from the cold waters and soon white from bleach buckets along the porches of the house.

One night we were gigging flounder in the sound, and I was walking next to him in shin-deep waters, shining the lantern to show the bi-clops eyes on the sandy, colored side of the fish lying on the floor below. Something sharp bit at my calves over and over; after the first few times I jumped, Tom told me it was shrimp leaping against my legs. I swung the lantern around and caught him stabbing me with the pronged tips of his gig every time I took a step. The expression on his face was more of pleasure than of worry for being caught.

It was at that unsettling house that my parents visited me for the first time since I had worked in tobacco fields. Upon discovering I was pregnant, my dad refused to speak to me while my mother began telling off the Buggers and insisting I get married. I had been out of their home and on my own for nearly nine years already, but I listened and soon found myself standing in front of a magistrate in Newport, next to this man smelling of wine from the night before, myself sporting a cut lip and reddened eyes, standing next to this man I knew I didn't love, and still taking his name. Though I never even uttered anything remotely linked to "I do" the magistrate announced the common law legal, and I almost passed out at his proclamation. Tom's oldest sister held onto me to prevent me from falling, while he was happily shaking hands and pouring more wine.

Despite our efforts to work at fishing and trading, during much of this time I took odd jobs to keep the rent paid—Tom usually drank up whatever we had, and I was responsible for the rent during those times. I began working as a maid for a military couple with two children and for a couple who had recently found their fortune in cable splicing for television. Their houses were pleasant and quiet, the military house always empty during my hours and full of children's messes and military paperwork, the cable-splicing house usually occupied by the woman of the house, who was very kind to me and often had me watch soaps or eat lunch with her to take up extra hours so she could pay me more. She must have been lonely despite their newfound wealth because she never wanted me to leave until her husband finished working.

Returning home was always uncomfortable, both physically and emotionally, so I continued taking refuge in the garden. At night I would enter the house and begin dinner. Not knowing whether Tom was coming home, I knew better than to not have a meal on the table if he did appear. Anyway, I still enjoyed cooking, the smell of fresh bread and vegetables, the taste of fish and scallops.

Before the pregnancy I'd never weighed over ninety pounds, but now I was told I needed to gain twenty-five pounds for the baby to be healthiest. I took extra care making sure the meals were balanced and quit smoking cigarettes, drinking, and even using caffeine—no coffee, no Pepsi, no Coke. I was dedicated to having the healthiest baby I could, but my physical condition wasn't perfect. Still recovering from injuries suffered in the embankment "accident," I had to be hospitalized several times during my first pregnancy because of complications, one of which was placenta previa, where the placenta moves to a lower position and causes bleeding.

I wasn't well. I had to appear at the doctor's office for daily esterol level checks and for a variety of other tests (some now considered much more commonplace, such as amniocentesis and ultrasound). I took my sewing with me and—never needing a pattern, the patterns imprinted in my hands from my mind—began to cut fake fur from a remnant store into the shapes of bears, lambs, and wild cats. I even cut a calf out of some brown spotted fur. It was easy.

On September 24, 1980, near the end of the eighth month of the pregnancy, I began experiencing contractions and other symptoms of early delivery. I had been at the doctor's office early that morning, worked as a maid until two o'clock in the afternoon, and toiled in the garden long enough to have a timber rattler spook me and my

English Setter. That afternoon the doctor called and, reporting that the esterol levels weren't good, asked me to come to his office on the back side of the hospital around seven o'clock in the evening. I packed a bag of sewing materials, Velcro I was sewing onto cloth diapers so I wouldn't have to use pins, a half-finished baby quilt, a lamb and a bear I was sewing eyes on already, a change of clothes, paper, pens, and a couple of books, just in case I wasn't coming back.

Somehow I knew I wasn't.

On the way to the hospital a storm roared in, blackening the sky and bringing hard rain. A hurricane just off the Carolina coast spun the clouds so, though the moon was full, it only peeked through the darkness.

Even though it was evening and the office was technically closed, my doctor had a few nurses on hand to assist in my examination. I liked him and was glad his wife, a midwife, assisted him. They had always let me hear the baby's heartbeat during visits, and this time began no differently. Just as the doctor was finishing up, the heartbeat vanished from our hearing and from the screen. The medical staff's faces went somehow, and panic came into the room.

"It's there," I insisted. "You're just missing it."

"Get her to surgery stat!"

The doctor explained that both the baby and I were in chronic distress, and he imagined either or both of us would not survive the surgery. The placenta had literally begun to break apart over the past few weeks and at this time had become full abruptia. I was being cut open before I was completely out, but I do remember uttering the honorable thing, the maternal line we have heard repeated enough times to know to say in this situation: "Forget me. Save the baby."

Five days later, I came to. When they brought in my new baby boy, Travis, from neonatal he was in an incubator and had his eyes bandaged. They removed the gauze for me to nurse him and told me he had arrived with his eyes wide open. Looking at him, his eyes truly looked like they already knew everything. Soon afterward, the hospital staff asked if I would be willing to express milk to feed preemies whose mothers could not or would not nurse them themselves. I agreed. Despite my own mother's lack of example, my maternal instincts were so strong, so heavy; I had enough milk for quadruplets.

Pumpkin, now living in San Francisco, visited while I was in the hospital, offering to give blood for my transfusions (which the hospital refused, just as they didn't believe she was my flesh-and-blood sister). Pumpkin had lactated slightly during my pregnancy even though we were living a few thousand miles apart. She and I came home on my release to find all the furniture moved back against the walls, the rugs rolled up, the entire house full of beer cans and wine bottles, and abandoned. Once everything was cleaned up, I brought in a laundry basket for Travis to sleep in when he wasn't in bed with me. Over the years, Pumpkin had become so urban that she was startled by crickets' chirps and leery of the complete darkness, so unlike San Francisco nights. Still into activism, social partying, and hanging out with her colleagues, she didn't stay long.

As soon as Travis was six weeks old, Tom would take the baby to his mother during the day while I was forced to go back to oystering. The ocean waters now frozen around the edges and snow drifts covering the islands, I put on the waders, went down into the waters, and lifted buckets full of oysters to him on board the skiff. Still recovering from the "accident" and now from the surgery and birth, my physical strength was truly a thing of the past; I grew ill and was shaking hard, my nose running. He would laugh at me when I asked for something to wipe the snot from my face, saying, "After *we* get twenty-five buckets up here *you* can have some Kleenex." And so, with snot running four inches down my face and recovering from the Cesarean, I picked oysters all winter in the ocean somewhere off the Outer Banks of the Carolinas.

Sometimes today when I'm down and remembering, it's still that cold and I still have a burden to load no matter where I am.

On those nights he did come home, I continued to pretend to be asleep so he'd hurt me less. Sometimes I'd force myself to sleep to ensure he was convinced. Sometimes in my dreams I was free.

> I dream someone is in the house and wants to take Travis. I pray that they leave him, and they reach toward me instead. I say that he needs me, and they ask for Tom. In this dream I agree to let him go, and when I awake I believe that it is real and that something lingers in this house, waiting

for opportunity. I am afraid for Tom but wish secretly that something would happen to him so I can go on with my own life. Sometimes I wish him death.

Not long after Travis's birth, we visited my parents. I sat in my dad's house while my brother and my man drank in the kitchen, arguing and threatening each other over who had the right to beat me up. The next day my brother beat up my mother again while my dad was working. Claiming I was going to pick up our commodities, I drove to the state elder abuse office over in Raleigh and told them the total circumstances surrounding the event. An intake worker would not believe my story. I returned to the house alone and moved all my brother's possessions onto the edge of the yard. When my dad came home, we locked my mother in her room so that she wouldn't let my brother back in and so that she wouldn't hit us while we were moving him out. When my brother pulled a gun on me, I called the police. The cops criticized me for "starting trouble," claiming that when I was away they never received any calls about my dad's place.

I guess not.

We moved to Mecklenberg County just south of Charlotte a short time later, where my man could find work (supposedly). This was Tom's country, urban guerrilla that he was, but he agreed to get a place out of town. Although the gesture was purportedly for me, I knew the living arrangement would make it difficult for me to know what he was up to when not home. By now, though, only he believed I cared.

We moved into a mobile home off a back road, where I stayed most of the time with my baby while his dad spent most of his time in Charlotte. Sometimes he would come back with cash register ink all over his arms and clothes, sometimes bloodied with someone else's blood, and almost all the time drunk and accompanied by friends. Obviously he was robbing again, and by the smell of gasoline on his clothes I assumed Tom was probably being hired for insurance arsons. I said nothing and left him to do whatever he wanted as long as he wasn't cuffing me. Once when he and his friends got out of hand I tried to run them out of the trailer. Getting pellet shot, I took a broom and laid out Tom's nose, but he just kept coming at me anyway, like there was nothing to stop him.

I dreamt of burning the trailer with him in it. I also began writing stories and sneaking up to Chapel Hill to record some of my songs in a studio.

On weekends Tom and his crew inevitably would fight somebody and somebody's cousins and brothers, resulting in death or in everybody's being rendered useless. Sometimes we would be in a car together, and they would all be clicking pistols while telling me where to drive so they could pop off rounds at enemies in North Charlotte. Once a friend of his who was a prison-guard baby of a chain-gang mother accompanied him and several others to fight some cousins somewhere; that friend came back with his guts in his hands from being cut but smiling and joking and laughing about whether the wound was serious enough to go to the hospital. Another time my man sat at the table playing cards and shot one of his "brothers" in the leg just for the hell of it, then laughed it off, saying, "Don't worry. We'll take you in as soon as this hand is over. Ante up."

On a weekend in the first spring after I had my baby, a war erupted between the next two trailers and ours. That conflict soon put a stop to everything but surviving. Many times I would take the baby and hold him underneath me on the floor to shield him from passing bullets. For days the fighting would break out, off and on during the day, then settle down again.

Enough was enough. I had no car and nowhere to go, yet one day I snapped, and without a conscious thought I yelled out for everyone to hold their fire. I walked out of the bullet-ridden trailer carrying nothing but the baby, walked down the dirt road, and never looked back. I kept going until I got to the highway, where I hitchhiked to Charlotte and called my sister from a pay phone.

Being personally unfamiliar with domestic violence, Pumpkin wasn't the easiest person for me to explain things to, but she was the only person I knew not living in alcohol and violence. Making her home in the state of California, she represented escape to me, the only one living far enough away so that my man couldn't find me and bring me back. After lecturing me for a while about the inconvenience

I would be in her life, she reluctantly agreed to send me a plane ticket, and I hitchhiked over to the airport to get on board.

1981. Having never flown before, I had no idea where to go or what to do, but I managed to end up on that plane with my baby and flew through three time zones to San Francisco. I caught my first cab ever into the city. At around one o'clock in the morning, walking alone with my baby tied to me, I reached Pumpkin's tenant building on the corner of Turk and Hyde in the Tenderloin District of San Francisco

Gunshots erupted below, outside a gay bar called 222 (which I dubbed the Triple Deuce), my first night in the city. Two people screamed about one stepping out on the other and fought. When I heard gunshots, my first reaction was to lay on the floor with the baby, but here the war was below us, and I didn't know what to do. I banged on Pumpkin's door, and she told me to go back to sleep, that it had nothing to do with us and would be over soon. She seemed dull to the street, but I didn't sleep and paced until morning.

Pumpkin was working as a printer for a paper. A union member for several years and an activist, she was very busy with rallies and other doings that she felt "I wouldn't understand." Walking and talking fast, moving with a purpose all the time, Pumpkin evoked memories of the city Skins who'd come around North Carolina in the early 1970s looking for support for political endeavors. She told me that if I was going to stay there I was responsible for cleaning and if I wanted to eat or get medical care I could go down to the mission.

Her half-side, Clay, was a Chicano/mestizo from Albuquerque, whom Pumpkin had met while living there and had talked into taking a ride with her when she moved to San Francisco. He wrote baseball stories and was one of the friendliest men I've ever known. Clay had visited with the painters of a mural on the Turk side of the building while they were working, probably sharing whatever he was drinking or smoking and talking baseball. A baseball was inserted in the middle of that mural, obviously having nothing to do with the painting's content but painted as a favor or tribute for Clay by the muralists. While Pumpkin was at work, Clay would sneak me food, and we would smoke cigars on the fire escape, watching the street like sentries.

Though culture shocked, I learned the city quickly by running errands and grocery shopping for Pumpkin, walking with a map in my pocket and a baby tied to my back. It was hard to believe so many people lived there on such a small piece of land, and San Francisco proved disorienting because the buildings were so high I lost sight of directional magnetism. North seemed south, and often there was sun only at midday.

The Tenderloin District was dangerous and interesting. Drive-by shootings weren't confined to Charlotte. Once when crossing Hyde Street to buy a pack of smokes, I flipped off a car whizzing past too close. The driver turned and unloaded a piece as I dropped to the street and watched people scatter at the sound. The bullet hit the wall on the side of the store across the corner, and I decided it would be a good idea to keep my finger in my fist while in the Tenderloin District. Nights were crazy there. Hookers frequented the corners, and immigrants unable to find housing slept on the sidewalks. If you were female and went to the store after dark, you had to tell the ladies you weren't in the business or they'd get fired up for your being on their corner. Sometimes their pimps would try to recruit you by asking, "Hey, come check out my ride." In the daytime many Asian families passed through; many thought Travis was Asian too. They would stop, click their tongues at him, and make such a fuss that he began getting upset when the Asian families didn't seem to notice him, and he'd clear his throat for attention.

Many homeless slept in the Tenderloin District, and it was sad to see how many were Indian. One old Native man had been there for years, and no one spoke his language or knew his history. During the years my sister lived in San Francisco, he went from walking to using a walker to disappearing completely. A lot of the city Skins would approach me—much like the guys back home—with a simply query: "Sister, got a cigarette?" Sometimes after I'd finished Pumpkin's chores, I'd share cigarettes and food and visit with them until the fog rolled in. I met a couple of Skins from the halfway house up Turk and felt comfortable with those living on the street because I'd done the same thing when I first left home.

I felt that Pumpkin was pretty ashamed of me. She'd completed high school and gone on to college and cities, working for newspa-

pers as she made her way across the country proofreading and print-
ing. Her vocabulary was far superior to mine, and she could always
put me in my place simply by outtalking me. When Pumpkin had
friends over, I'd try to keep up with the conversations, but she'd put
me down and say things like, "She's from the sticks. All she knows is
how to make trinkets. She'll end up selling trinkets to tourists on the
side of the road one day. Don't bother telling her things because she
won't understand." Most of her friends seemed friendly, but with this
introduction and the obvious differences in the sophistication of our
language, they'd usually talk real slow and treat me like I was slow
minded.

Still, I believe Pumpkin had good intentions, but she just couldn't
"see" me. She was a product of my mother's insanity and our childhood relationships tightly bound by dysfunction, and her idea of
helping was to "educate" me as to how hard the world could be—
completing household chores, effectively carrying out our mother's
crusade for me to be "responsible," scrubbing her toilet and baseboards, and carrying the load. Though we were sisters, we derived
from separate worlds, differentiated by our mother's classification of
us as children and the divergence of our life experiences.

I was raising Travis, but nothing in my life had prepared me to
know what to do with babies. Everything I did was by instinct alone.
Once my baby caught red measles, ended up in the St. Francis Hospital emergency room, and didn't move for three days. I had always
been concerned about his health because he'd come in with difficulty
and been diagnosed with mild cerebral palsy with some heart problems not long after birth. He was rigid, so stiff you didn't have to work
to bundle him; when most babies begin to sit up on their own, Travis
started to bend enough to be placed in a sitting position. Even so, he
was always active and moving, the kind of baby that usually scooted
across the crib at two weeks. It was thus scary to see him so still and so
hot with the measles. After I brought him home, one morning I went
down on the street and bought some red carnations for a couple of
bucks and put them in the window facing Turk. When Travis began
to come out of the measles fever, the carnations were the first things
that caught his attention. Once he reached out toward them I knew
he would survive.

Once he recovered, Pumpkin took us to see the Pacific, a hard ocean, full of stiff waves and unforgiving. I had no desire to fish these waters too ruined by the populations flooding the Bay Area. That evening we took a cruise over to Alcatraz on some coupons she'd saved and were pleased we could make out "Indians Welcome" in fading red paint from the Indian activist occupations I'd only heard about through word of mouth before. On the tour we were told that the prison was originally built to house prisoners of war. Indian prisoners. Leaders of the Modocs and warriors with courage, fighting only to remain free in their own lands. An internment prison. We left depressed at what we learned but heartened that some had taken a stand on those issues years ago when we were young.

Problems began to mount for me in San Francisco. I applied for social services after I'd been in the Tenderloin District a month. Where I was from it was easy to get commodities, WIC, and food stamps; in San Francisco, social workers investigated before making a final decision. The worker who came to see our place reported that I had no furniture and judged this as evidence of transience. They closed the case without ever allowing me any benefits; I appealed and won only food stamps. Pumpkin demanded I pay her rent, but I could not find work.

I stayed in the city until I got a call saying that Tom was possibly mortally wounded in Charlotte General Hospital and wanted to see his son. Pumpkin was quite happy to put me on a plane and ship me back, making me fill out an IOU for the two plane tickets she'd paid for. I flew back without thinking much about it.

Looking back, it is evident I was following my father's path in attempting to provide stability for someone desperately lost, swept into a whirlpool of misguided loyalty without an oar to still the pull. I now recognize the similarity between my mother and my man: the tight tangle of reality surrounded by gross magnitudes of delusion, the only significant difference being that his impulse was self-invoked by alcohol and hers was unexplainable. Not surprisingly, Tom in the past had denied that my mother could really be insane and even tried to convince me she was onto something everyone else might have missed. The twenty-two-year-old mother who returned to North

Carolina that day had watched her dad endure her mother's decades of insanity, and that relationship provided a measure of normalcy for her own. I also believed that, if I did truly leave, Tom would find and kill me or get me back anyway. No matter what, I was still accountable and a hostage in mind and flesh. So, I figured, it made little difference. I didn't remember the easy way to leave.

In fact, it was easy to believe Tom was dying in the hospital—his face mangled as he'd often done to mine, skull suffering from multiple fractures, nose bleeding so uncontrollably it had to be cauterized repeatedly. When I brought our baby to the intensive care unit, Tom cried and begged me to stay with him, promising that if he lived everything would be different and he would quit drinking and straighten up.

Everyone had an opinion about our relationship. Tom's uncle and brother-in-law gave me a hard time for leaving him, claiming that when I was with him he did all right but when I left it came to this (as if Tom never had problems before he met me). My mother called, insisting that because he was the father of my son I should help him and stay with him. Tom's friend whose guts had lain in his own hands a while back told me, however, that Tom had gotten injured on purpose to get me back; apparently he had tried to snag the wrong man's woman, a fight ensued, and he did not defend himself. The friend confided that I was being set up and that if I stayed Tom would eventually kill me.

It was hard, though, not to pity the father of your child when he was in the violent injuries ward of Charlotte General Hospital. I agreed to stay for the time he was in the hospital but declared I would be leaving when he recovered. Unfortunately, he didn't heal up when released; his nose would begin to gush blood, and someone had to get him medical attention to be cauterized so he wouldn't bleed to death. After his nose was burned so many times that the bleeding finally stopped, he agreed to go with me over the ridge to Tennessee to try to begin a different way of living. Tom kept crying and promising he'd changed. I wanted desperately to believe that there is good in everybody and that he should have a chance to father the boy we'd had. I wanted to believe so much that I figured maybe we just needed to leave everything we knew behind and to hope that a move would change things.

We picked Nashville—I don't remember for what reason other than record labels and hope for recording opportunities—and we found a place on Sweetbriar in an older section of town that was an all-Black community except for us. Three of us and three dogs (I still had two setters and the sheltie I'd been with since the age of eight) lived on the top floor of a house surrounded by huge yards with plenty of room for the dogs outside. I found work at a department store, and Tom started washing cars for the police department—of all places. I think he could con his way into anything. That was his true gift, conning.

Tom was sober and offered to paint the entire house for the landlord in lieu of a couple of months' rent, so our lives seemed promising at first. Clay and Pumpkin came to visit on their way east. It was a good visit, but I was sick and gaining weight. She teased me about being pregnant, but I was sure it was the flu and stress because no other changes had occurred to indicate pregnancy. I got tested anyway and found I was more than four months along already.

With that news, Tom began staying out later than he worked, coming home drunk with the off-duty cops, who would stand for him and blame themselves for his being late—as if I cared. They would leave and he would cuff me up. No matter the opinion of relatives, I knew at this point that there was no redeeming him. Becoming increasingly heavy, I was once carrying Travis and having difficulty climbing an iced-over, wooden-plank staircase on the side of the house leading to our door. Anxious not to be late to work, Tom shoved me down the entire flight of stairs to get me out of his way so he could get to the police station on time.

My sixteen-year-old sheltie died there, his kidneys failing and starving him. I had him put down at the vet. He knew. He looked at me as they took him into the office, his eyes so sad with the knowledge I had to let him go. I picked him up an hour later and buried him under the wooden staircase.

Months later my dad called me at work—we had no phone at home—to report that he'd had a heart attack and that my brother had broken

his jaw and beaten up my mother because there wasn't enough mustard on his hot dog. Tom and I packed up and headed back to North
Carolina to move out my brother. I was thinking further ahead, however, hoping also to dump this man of mine in the process.

Moving my brother out was even harder now, since he had accumulated an arsenal of firearms and everybody was afraid of him.
Again we locked my mother in a room to keep her from fighting us.

At one point she screamed, "Don't you kick out my boy!"

My dad stopped, looked at her, and said quietly, "It's him or me. I
could move back to the Plains with Allison and leave you both here."

Looking up like a small child, my mother asked meekly, "Would
you write to me?"

Laughing, my father explained to me, "See, I can't leave her. She'd
let him beat her to death if she was left here." It was true. There was
nothing to convince her that he was dangerous. Suddenly I understood why so many times the mother of a mass murderer claims her
son couldn't possibly be guilty of any crime—craziness.

We then moved my brother's stuff on the street, and Tom took off
to drink somewhere. My brother returned, broke a window to get in,
loaded up a shotgun, and stuck it in my mouth in front of Travis. My
baby was by now about twenty months old, and I was about seven
months pregnant with a second child. Standing there, not flinching,
I stared right back at my brother. There was no way I could defend
myself if he released the trigger.

Laughing, he suddenly lowered the shotgun and called the cops
to report me. They appeared to remove me from the house, leveling
accusations that I had only returned to cause trouble again, repeat-
ing that no one called them unless I was there and seeming to agree
with my brother that pregnant women were overly emotional. My
dad fortunately entered the room at that point and, as the property
owner, asked the police to get my brother's things and escort him out
of the house. Seething, my brother promised to kill every one of us
one day.

Older and newer currents of my life began to converge at this point,
these changes eventually moving me forward and away. Still dis-
traught over my sheltie dying, I ran ads to give away my last two dogs

(who were around ten years old) so I wouldn't have to go through losing them as well. Tom and I got a house in the older section of Cary, which by then had begun growing beyond a two-stoplight town. Really needing work to pay rent until I had the second baby, I somehow (with no degree and no teaching experience) landed a position to teach 3-D arts and songwriting in a visiting artist program called Special Performing Arts and Cultural Events, or SPACE.

Walking into my first class, held after school in a cafeteria alongside four other arts programs, I felt purposeful for the first time in years. Teaching felt as natural as fieldwork—I loved it. I told the students everything I'd ever wanted to hear from my teachers but didn't, praising them at every opportunity. We left class happily fulfilled and creatively inspired. I also had a chance to teach at the same juvenile center that had confined me years ago.

I was turning my life around. Myself.

Feeling hopeful again, I turned my attention to fixing up the house we'd rented. I scrubbed the tile in the house until you could see the pattern and then kept at it until the linoleum shone. Tom started up a house-painting business, and we painted our house inside and out with leftover paint from his work. My mother was ecstatic—finally I was keeping books for a husband with a business, her largest life dream for me. I set up a room for Travis and the baby on the way; for myself I planted a small garden out back where the land stretched to a tree line and to the sundown at evening.

I went into labor, and again there were complications: the baby was in fetal distress and I wasn't dilating. A Cesarean was performed, and, given an epidural and mirrors, I watched the whole surgery in reflections. Though I'd been told it was a girl following an ultrasound months before, four days before my twenty-fourth birthday my second boy was born around the same time of night I'd had my first. This time, though, both of us were pretty healthy afterward. I named my baby boy for Grandpa Vaughan. He looked a lot like my dad. It's a little scary to give birth to someone who looks like your elder.

Tom never showed up at the hospital.

My sister came to help, even though she knew absolutely nothing about kids. I told her to lock the doors up when she went to sleep. Pumpkin meant well in coming to help and tried to do whatever my son wanted her to do. Because she fed Travis every time he said "eat"—his favorite word—after only five days in the hospital none of Travis's clothes fit anymore. I barely recognized the guy when I got home because he was so round.

A while later, Travis needed a bath, but I wasn't supposed to lift anything after my surgery. Walking around the house, he carried my father's World War II man-sculpture with ivory eyes in his arms and called it his "baby." That hard-as-iron wooden man that my son found loveable I had been afraid of in the dark of my early childhood. Pumpkin was sleeping and Tom had come home, and I asked both of them to help me lift him into the tub. They ignored me, so I did it myself. A baseball-size swelling appeared at the incision immediately, and I called the doctor to ask what was happening. He said it was probably an incision hernia and told me that I wouldn't be able to have surgery to repair it for about a year. As I turned to tell off Tom and Pumpkin for not helping, Tom slammed me out before I could even utter a word. Pumpkin locked herself in a room while Tom cuffed me and the babies cried.

I told him to leave. He said he would if he had some money.

"How much?" I demanded.

He retorted, "Fifty bucks," glaring like this new threat he'd dreamed up would scare me.

In two minutes I called my dad to come bring fifty bucks and then paid Tom to get out. I was glad he was gone. But it wasn't for long.

When Vaughan was two weeks old, Pumpkin went back to work in California. Alone with two babies, I was luckily employed and the rent was paid up in advance. I stayed and worked teaching arts and writing workshops until Vaughan was about six months old.

Tom showed up. Unexpected, uninvited, he just walked in, sat down, and took over the house again. Ignoring his presence no matter how he provoked me or tried to make up, I refused to speak or react. But then he hit one of my babies. Travis saw him drinking a beer at the kitchen table and tried to imitate him, picking up the beer can like he was going to drink. His dad's hand came hard across his cheek.

Grabbing Travis out of his high chair, I started packing, although it took me two more months to save money to travel. During that time, I left most of my belongings packed by the door just to remind myself not to back out and stay. Tom started to try to go with me but backed out at the last minute.

I rented a trailer miles out into the country above Nashville and paid up the rent for three months. The place smelled like urine; evidently babies had lived in the trailer before. I walked up the road and called my grandfather in Canada, who promised me a home if I could get there. I called my family and asked for help to leave, but no one could help us.

The first night in the trailer I made a horrifying discovery. It was infested with wharf rats, twelve inches long and larger, monstrous rats that literally stood on their hind legs and danced because they were so delusional and ridden with disease. Each night they poured in, slinking through the walls and floors, looking for opportunity to feed. Night after night I fought and fought them, wielding a claw hammer, a glass two-liter Coke bottle, and huge traps laced with commod peanut butter hidden under paper in cardboard boxes. It was full-scale, full-blown war. Staring into their eyes and commanding them to leave my children alone, I may have looked fierce but I surely felt sheer terror. They ruled that place; it was their den. We survived there, I swear, solely on courage and prayers. I moved out as soon as possible, but without money and not knowing one person in the state, it didn't happen overnight. By the time we left we'd already contracted disease from the insidious creatures. All three of us were hospitalized, near death, and are lucky to be here today. The only thing that kept me breathing was thinking of my little ones and fearing no one in my family would find them if I couldn't pull through. I was driven and did not give in.

Once we were strong enough, my boys and I moved into a few more places before settling, for a while staying with Johnny Paycheck's drummer, Jack Smith, and his mixed-blood wife, Susan, who sang backup for Bill Anderson, I think. I filed for divorce with the help of an attorney from our own tribe, Linda Fizer, and began writing songs with one of Buffie St. Marie's former guitarists, Danny Ray.

Life was easier on our own, and we eventually moved west of Ashland City about ten miles to a house on Tanya Tucker's property called Tuckahoe, where I took care of a little girl for a couple who'd just moved there. It was beautiful—a pond glimmered directly in front of my place, and the Harpeth River flowed just up the road. A safe place. The country house was the nicest I'd ever slept in. It was clean, with waxed and shiny hardwood floors, a new stove and re- frigerator, and a garage big enough for cars and tractors. It even had a dishwasher—the first I'd seen—and something above the regular oven called a confection oven. Both appliances intimidated me so much that I never dared try to operate them.

The best thing about that house was its peacefulness and quiet surroundings. The road was far up the dirt path, and no one came down to our house but the employer. We were growing stronger, well away from towns, nearer to mounds from the old people, and along rivers with painted caves and fields full of deer. We knew we were home, really. The kids hung out with me while I composed songs and painted. They both wrote their own songs; Travis's inspirational lyrics called for people to understand each other, and Vaughan wrote his first blues song (claiming to be "on his own") here while still a toddler.

I was happy here, but since I was working for full-blood white people and they were very particular about their little girl, I knew it wouldn't last long. We were just too different. I made the best of our time there and fished almost every evening with my little ones at the pond out front.

Upon moving in, I had a dream that my grandpa was trying to call from Canada. I saw my grandma behind him, holding a blue stone necklace out toward me and apologizing for being cruel to me. Smil- ing, Grandpa said he was sorry for all I'd been through, and I knew he was dead. I drove to a pay phone, but his line was busy for hours. I called my mom and sister and asked them to call Aunt Nancy in Cal- gary to check it out. They broke into Grandpa's place and found him passed away with the phone in his hand and the phone book turned to the page for the hospital. My mom and sister went to the funeral, and afterward they called to say Grandma and Grandpa had left me some necklaces. When I asked about the blue one, they admitted no one had ever seen it before and asked how I knew about it. I shared the dream, and they mailed me a beaded rosette from Grandpa and the blue stone necklace from Grandma. I put away the necklace, accepting the gift as an apology, and I forgave her.

I began suffering from extreme nightmares that the children's father would show up and brutalize me to death.

And then the buzzards arrived. Once we saw what I thought were wild turkeys out back by the owner's spotted donkeys. I took the kids out to see them. Vaughan had just begun to walk and be weaned and was at the age of complete innocence and mobile. As he ran toward the turkeys, happy and smiling, I suddenly sensed danger and malice. The "turkeys" began leaving their "roosts" and moving in closer to the ground in unison, moving in closer to Vaughan ahead of me now by several yards. I dashed forward, scooped him up, grabbed Travis in the same rush, and turned to face a flock of buzzards.

Interpreting the buzzards' visit as an omen, I made plans to leave this job as soon as notice came. I vowed that I would live to raise my children no matter what misfortunes we might endure. I was certain I would be there for them until they could completely fend for themselves in the world. I had to be.

It was now 1984. Pumpkin called me from San Francisco after talking with my dad and asked me to represent (and record for) our family at the Red Clay Gathering of the Eastern and Western bands. I had been involved with various Native rallies since I was a kid but hadn't had experience with formal politics and was broke. Beadwork and baskets paid for our gas, food, and film. I spoke little during the gathering, being too shy in public. When approached or asked, however, I would talk about my family and look for relations in the crowd. I met Wilma Mankiller at the Red Clay Gathering and was impressed by her, by her strength and support during the four days I spent there.

My family's blood relatives attended, as did my kids' relatives from their other side, from whom I kept my distance. I met some distant relatives living on the Northern Plains who invited me to come out "anytime." Making a mental note of the invitation, I focused my attention on the Eternal Flame carried here by runners, one on the Walker side of the family, a blood relative, and I was proud. Seeing the fire encased made me both happy and sad that tourists would see this fire, and I wanted to protect it from them somehow, protect everything here. I took great care what I wrote for the record.

When I returned to Ashland City, the local paper featured on the front page an article on the gathering I wrote and my photographs. I was satisfied with the byline and coverage, but they cut out significant political statements and opinion and invented incorrect blurbs beneath photographs. This was my second newspaper publication and the first with photographs. I didn't want to draw negative attention to the gathering, so I didn't bother arguing with the paper.

True to my forewarning, my boss said he didn't think we were a good match for his little girl, so we moved again, this time into the basement of a house up on the highway north of town, about the time a massive flood overflowed the town below. Here I put in a full acre garden and worked it with Travis, who sang to the bees when they swarmed the baby until they were pacified and left. I resumed painting, mostly watercolors that looked like pastels, and also took pictures whenever I could afford film. My interest in trying to do something with creative writing in addition to songwriting led me to take performing arts classes at Nashville's Poverty Playhouse and Circle Theater. There I learned about scriptwriting. I was also busy teaching workshops in schools and for community programs.

One day in the Bluebird Café, Gary Lamb, a great-grandson of the circus performer the great Zambini, offered me a five-figure contract to produce me if I decided to perform. He was producing the band Chicago and the television show *Flamingo Road*. I laughed him off, not trusting white people with money who tried to "buy" me. He tried to wine and dine me to convince me he was sincere, but I told him I had a floor to mop and kids to feed and was too busy to have drinks and make deals. That was the greatest amount of money ever offered to me, well beyond what I could fathom. It was the second time in my life I had been offered a way out of what I knew, but I could not imagine myself owned by anybody.

I continued to flourish creatively, writing, managing to get some music published and recorded, and cowriting a children's show and a show called *Bluegrass to Blues* with Danny Ray for cable television. By the time the children were old enough to start preschool, I decided to follow my sister to California, where she claimed the kids would be better educated and I could continue taking classes, because "in California the first two years of college are free."

Before leaving Tennessee, Tom wrote to me. His family called my family to report that he was hospitalized again with multiple injuries. I finally knew better—if I returned to North Carolina I wouldn't live very long. I wasn't so worried about myself, but now I had two kids to think of, and I didn't want them anywhere near my brother or their dad. I knew we would always be tied to our peoples' lands, where our ancestors had been born, shed blood, and were buried, but I also knew it would be years before I could ever move back to stay. Our original lands reached much farther than the imposed statehood boundaries encompassed anyway.

Calling Tom's mother, I made my decision clear: "He has been successful in killing parts of me that committed no crime, in beating me, and in mentally and emotionally treating me so severely. I have tried to the best of my ability to be good to him and have done nothing against any of you. I have been forced to escape for my life and my children's lives to be spared his wrath, and I do not intend to come home again. If it means I must leave North Carolina for good, then this is how it will be."

After agonizing over letting people down, I finally got the courage to call my own family to explain. I remember telling my dad that I wasn't stone, the rock he always expected me to be, and that I just couldn't stay with someone crazy enough to kill me.

Chuckling a little, my father replied, "I never wanted you to be a rock. I wanted you to learn from the willow—to bend with bad winds but retain yourself."

"Oh."

I had never felt so stupid. Here I had spent all this time working on duty and loyalty to the craziest influences in my life, and now I discovered I had the wrong philosophy about responsibility all along. But as always, my father's words rang true and were meaningful. I still had a lot to learn about people and living well.

With the split obviously final, we left for the West Coast, but after our first stay we ended up heading to the Northern Plains in a loaded truck, staying there until Travis was almost ready for kindergarten. He never did go to Headstart, but he began kindergarten in the fall of 1985 in Santa Paula, California, after another brief stay in San Francisco with my sister. Though we didn't have much money, the kids always had clothes and toys. They were rummage really but clean, and the kids were still too young to know the difference. I was devoted to giving my kids more opportunity than I had and asked Pumpkin for advice.

Pumpkin thoroughly convinced me that most of my problems were because of lack of education. She claimed my eighth grade and GED education weren't enough and that the noncredit classes I'd taken at NCSU didn't count because they were traditional arts studies and didn't relate to jobs in the "real" world.

How would I fit into a world based on professions and incomes? I thought of my former uncle-in-law, William, of the knowledge he had of fieldwork, fishing, and living simply, of how "educated" he was in his "fields" of expertise with his third-grade education, and how he had gotten by just fine with the exception of his addiction to alcohol. My father (who was of higher education thanks to the World War II GI Bill, determination, and fence riding) raised me to continue the work and philosophical process begun long before his own time. Most of what I learned from Dad balanced incorporating his scientific knowledge with his congenital and traditional knowledge, and I could scarcely imagine learning more from any other human being.

Cornered by my past and confused by the future, I recalled my mother praising my sister's intelligence. Feeling less than adept at understanding people, I couldn't imagine fitting into a true urban environment on a long-term basis, something my sister mastered easily. I had no idea how to get by without a garden, without a place to fish or hunt, without time to quilt, bead, or carve. I worried out loud about losing those parts of me and how that loss would affect the upbringing of my children. Pumpkin insisted I couldn't understand because I was too backward. ("Those ways are gone," she'd say, "gone." Or, when insisting I go to college for credit, she'd ask, "What are you going to do? Sell trinkets on the side of the road?")

Every time I asked her why people are the way they are, why human beings continually use and abuse each other, why compassion is seen as a weakness, why loyalty is deemed old-fashioned and foolish, why hardly anyone is living up to the standards our Native traditions laid out for us to live by, she would simply say, "Almost 500 years of oppression—that's why." Her philosophy seemed to assume that no one ever had to answer to personal responsibility at any time—unless it was me. I thought that she regarded me as foolish for believing there was more to life than politics, deceit, and death.

All I could think at the time was that no one ever beat Pumpkin; in fact, I had fought *for* her. So I figured she knew something I didn't, maybe lots of things. She was my older sister and worldly, devoting her lifework to activism, her occupation to the written word. I respected and mostly believed her opinions, and I wanted my own family to survive, wanted my own kids to have a better shot than I'd had. When we moved, my boys and I crossed a continent, ocean to ocean.

ALONE WALKING

There
has always
been no one
when
there most
definitely
should have
been   someone
here   to ease
hardships
endured   thru
this walk
and someone
could   have
definitely
been   there
when
no one
always   was
there

    from *Dog Road Woman*

7

Crossings

My Huron grandmas (Lucy and Paulina) were more than familiar with canoeing prior to meeting their French-Canadian men (Tremblais and Gervaisse), both sailors and traders. For a while they traveled, fought, and worked on waterways from Quebec to New York, to Michigan, and to Illinois. For an entire generation they migrated back and forth on waters before eventually moving south and settling in Indian Territory. Together they sought places where the family could utilize their strengths and survive the times. But when one of our Tsa la gi grandmas, Betsy (Bessie) Walker, was forced to leave her homeland on foot, we were told she was separated from her family and she walked alone.

I remember the story my dad told of our grandma Betsy Walker. She'd been captured by American soldiers in North Carolina, alone with some of her children, and forced to walk to what became Oklahoma, dying along the way. Captive once before in childhood by an enemy tribe, she had made her way back home as a young woman to marry one of her own people, but this permanent removal from the homeland was too hard to bear. They said that the pain of leaving forever grieved her heart and that loss crossed her over.

I remember how her children were said to be divided: the ones in North Carolina eventually becoming known for their expert horsemanship and other talents, those in Oklahoma forced to learn to live in a strange land, completely on their own. They knew who they were and where they came from, and they adapted to and adopted Indian Territory as their own. They reorchestrated their lives, keeping their beliefs and their hearts protected, changing but surviving still.

Looking out a eastward window, while for the first time witnessing the sunrise over sacred Chumash mountains, red and purpled, home to deer, bear, puma, margay, and condors, high over green desert palms, I remember Grandma Betsy and her children in my prayers before cooking pancakes, cornmeal, and eggs for my own little ones. My wish for the day is to find the place of peace for myself and my kids.

A few moments later, my youngest son comes running downstairs, smiling and so excited he can barely stand still, saying, "Travis, gonna fly!"

"Where's Travis going to fly to?" I ask, wiping my hands on a dish towel and facing him.

"Out the window," he says, still smiling and all happy, turning to run back upstairs to see.

I follow and find my four-year-old perched on the bedroom windowsill, smiling as happily as his brother and completely lined with hawk feathers Scotch-taped to his shoulders, back, and in staggered rows down both his arms. Feathers usually kept in a box near my beading materials and a personal collection of rough rocks and smooth stones on a desk next to the kitchen table. Feathers that now make his tiny thin body appear birdlike.

Looking at him perched there, what first flashes in my mind are all the times Travis *perched* instead of sitting, on chairs, on the porch, on fence tops, everywhere, even to the point of running to jump in a pond of water, then perching and hopping in at the last moment. I now see that he literally feels birdlike and believes he can fly and will try if I don't interfere. I also realize that if I make the wrong move he might fall out the window anyway since the boys have removed the screen entirely and his toes are already curled far over the outer edge.

"Travis, could you come dust off the cabinets so I can cook?" I ask.

He turns toward me, looks out the window again, and hops down, saying, "Okeh."

All the way downstairs he tells me of his flying dreams and how he wants to fly up to those mountains we can see from our bedroom windows, to see if they look like mountains at home in North Carolina and Tennessee, to see if they run with rivers, bear, and deer. Vaughan repeats whatever Travis says to me.

We have traveled so much in so little time I, too, understand that sense of soaring he yearns for, that sea-level avoidance, making motion toward higher, safer, wooded grounds. At nights here in yet another strange land, I often dream of flying. The flight, however, is much more fight than soar, my body moving like struggling small birds in flight, pulling wind and pushing feathered matter onward, yearning to soar but too busy fending off larger birds and rivals to glide.

I long for a quiet hill somewhere myself. All of us do.

I remember the story of how my dad's mother's Huron/French-Canadian family left Quebec, migrating south through the states, then west, ending up in Indian Territory, where they blended in with recently relocated Wyandottes and Cheyennes. Eventually she settled in Cloud Chief, Oklahoma, where more of her brothers and sisters would be born, and from there she would meet my grandfather. How different Oklahoma was from the Woodlands of all our eastern origins. In this generation we are still locked into migration patternings, as if moving crisscross from original to migratory ancestral homes and back would somehow manage to enable us to maintain identity despite oppressive abuses and traumas making crossings themselves over our familial paths.

I sometimes wonder what yearnings stayed with my ancestral relations as they resettled in Oklahoma, in Texas, stayed in all the relocated lives. I know they were all too busy trying to survive to let themselves sicken thinking about what they left behind. Their moves were only the sad results of another people's push for greed, for control—mineral, waterway, and land. Our own current move to California itself was another of the consequences of the gifts of alcohol and abuse made on a traditionally philosophical people, a people who came into this earth by help from the water beetle bringing earth from below the waters under the Sky-Vault and by Buzzard flapping his mighty wings to form the very mountains of our people's home, a home we were far away from now.

It was 1985, I was in my late twenties, and we had just moved to California strictly on my sister's suggestion. Not knowing anybody else and unable to live in the city like Pumpkin, I literally put my finger on a map and found a small town named Santa Paula. I drove there and rented a duplex apartment the same day. The town was populated by mostly Mexicans at that time along with some Chumash families, some whites, and a few Asians and Blacks. It seemed familiar — brown-faced people sauntering to the grocery or to Laundromats to wash the field dirt from their clothing after picking citrus in the surrounding fields. Encircled by mountains and peaceful, Santa Paula would do just fine.

I taught art and writing classes, and upon the recommendation of a teacher I auditioned for and was accepted at the intermediate level in a performing arts school in Los Angeles. I drove the ninety miles back and forth to Los Angeles, perhaps the only person not angered by jams and construction delays; I just played tapes and waited it out.

The people of Hollywood, of entertainment in general, might as well have been from one of my mother's delusions, as little as I understood them, and it was fairly obvious they felt the same about me. When I began performing arts classes, I heard wannabe ingénues say, "She doesn't belong here" and "She sounds like a real hick." I didn't and I was.

Bouts of incredible stage fright sometimes paralyzed me. Our voice instructor from Oklahoma wrote in my report, "Almost too shy to sing," a telling remark because I loved to sing when alone or with family and friends. Luckily, there were other Skins at the school, making it easier to socialize. A young guy from Oklahoma, Grant Brittan, knew some of my extended relations, and a Jemez Pueblo, Ernie Fragua, worked in the office and made our transition and stay as comfortable as possible (most of the other Indians attending were much more familiar with cities already).

One Native urban beauty trying to start her motorcycle outside had trouble with the electric starter, so I kick-started it for her. Afterward Derya and I became friends, and I became friends with her father, Dehl, too. They were mixed of Apache descent and nonstatus, like me. Dehl was from Pueblo, Colorado, and his family hailed from New Mexico (born Eduardo Carrillo). Orphaned as a young boy, he had made his own way in life from the age of thirteen. I was inspired by his success in the performing arts and in his personal life and found him to be supportive of me as well as many other emerging writers, artists, and performers. Dehl was involved with the

American Indian Registry for the Performing Arts and encouraged me to join. Derya's mother was from Turkey, so she was of Middle-Eastern culture as well. It felt good having a family I could visit with here; though their lifestyles were quite different from mine, they were good-hearted people.

I was mostly interested in studying performing arts because I was interested in writing script. I believed it would be essential to writing good script to better understand how actors worked. I also felt that the stereotypes of Hollywood Indians could only be changed by Indigenous writers. More First Nations performers also deserved to work in the industry. Indian children need good role models in their surroundings, including what was pumped into their homes electronically. Reading and interpreting script improved my vocabulary. When I came across any new word or name, I would immediately research it thoroughly to ensure adequate interpretation of the dialogue.

I soon found that writing monologues for auditioning performers could be lucrative. Having picked up an old Royal typewriter at a local rummage sale for five bucks, I began writing personalized monologues to fit an actor's range and ability. Fees from such ghostwritten monologues funded good portions of my rent several times.

Another benefit was the ability to cry again after years of withholding emotion. I was required to cry on cue during a performance of *Danny and the Deep Blue Sea* with Angelo Michael Masino. I had to literally learn to cry with my older sister's coaching. It opened a floodgate, and I was at once free. Later, I reorchestrated Masino's play, *Queens, New York*, as the replacement director. It was a success, though the trade papers neglected to credit me at all, not realizing the changes they lauded were mine. Nothing here to cry about—these things happen.

My greatest challenge during those first months in California was physical. I was diagnosed with a rare variety of squamous-cell carcinoma soon after the move. After praying about it, I immediately went into surgery and had the carcinoma removed. A couple of weeks later, however, I had a new growth and required more surgery. My doctor said that this particular type never goes away, reoccurring so often that I would most likely have to be examined every twelve weeks for the rest of my life. In addition, I began suffering from episodes of uncontrollable shaking, clumsiness, blackouts, visual disturbances, unusual repetitive behaviors, severe stuttering or "drunk talk" while completely sober, sudden blindness, and deafness, often occurring during performances, which I was told were related to eye migraines and stress. I had experienced spasmodic episodes and a slight tremor all my life, and I remembered blacking out several times before, but most of the symptoms were new (it would take many years, a steady progression of episodic maladies, and another hard knock on the head causing my first grand mal, or tonic clonic seizure, before I would be diagnosed with complex partial/temporal lobe epilepsy). In the performing arts school at that time, I only knew that my extreme fear of urban crowds, public speaking, and performance often resulted in bouts of impediment and confusion. I toughed it out, managing eventually to earn a professional certificate in the course.

About the time I was settling into classes, a Big Mountain benefit was held in Ventura, about fifteen miles away from Santa Paula. As one of the organizers, I invited Dehl to speak since he was an established actor in the industry. Mostly we had a good evening. Some excellent bands, drum groups, and speakers appeared—Floyd Westerman and the boys prior to an even larger Big Mountain benefit scheduled in Los Angeles for the following weekend with John Trudell, Jesse Ed Davis, and Charlie Hill—and mostly local Indian and Latino families showed up for the feed. The event was held at a Veterans of Foreign Wars building, with a bar adjoining the main room, so some people were crossing over to drink by the time the event was coming to a close.

A mestizo man I was seeing at the time, Manuel, got loaded, ran into some old friends, and wanted to leave in my car. We debated in the parking lot, he attempting to grab my keys when seemingly out of nowhere around eight cops jumped out and sicked dogs on Manuel, throwing him to the ground to get him in handcuffs. Preconditioned to deal with excessive force from police, I slipped back into the vfw building and made it through a police barricade by lying on the floor of an organizer's car.

When Manuel's case came to jury trial I was a main witness, as was my older friend Dehl. When Dehl took the stand, he likened the arrest to roping a calf and vouched for the unnecessary use of excessive force and racism. The judge made racist comments not only about Indian people but about anyone he could refer to as "those people," including Armenians (which coincidentally identified the governor of California at the time). Writing down every inappropriate comment the judge made during the proceedings, I logged them with the public defenders assigned to the case, then pulled records to find out how many of the arresting cops had a history of excessive force on their record.

During the trial I wrote notes to the public defenders with questions for them to ask the cops, Manuel, and Dehl. By the time I took the stand I was happy to tell the truth because it was increasingly evident that the arrest sprang from racially motivated surveillance by the local police. After uncovering enough records to prove wrongful intent by the cops, we felt we had a good chance for justice to be served and for an innocent verdict. At this point one of the public defenders wrote me a note: "You did an outstanding job. You should go to law school." The jurors read an innocent verdict, citing misdoings of the police, but the judge shocked everyone by chastising the jury, calling them crazy for their decision, and imposing a work order on top of an innocent verdict.

Immediately researching who was in charge of judges through my activist sister in San Francisco, I called the Judicial Performance Committee in Sacramento, reported the judge's actions and behavior, and then mailed my trial notes and a letter describing what I relayed on the phone. The judge's work order was immediately revoked, and spies were sent into his courtroom over the next few weeks. Soon he was removed from the bench; grateful public defenders later told us that the judge was manic-depressive and that they had tried unsuccessfully for months previous to this trial to have him investigated to no avail. This was the only political coup I can claim sole responsibility for.

Maybe six months after we moved to Santa Paula, Travis began kindergarten. He was so physically weak he couldn't handle the walk to school without resting on the curb several times. Not understanding California kids, he played alone quite happily. One day, though, I received a call from the school that some kids had been picking on him, thinking he was Spanish but not speaking the language. They were calling him "Pocho" and ridiculing him. The teacher was worried because Travis had isolated himself on the far side of the playground in a swarm of bees. Going to the school, I called him over and asked what he was doing.

"The bees are my friends," he assured me. "They won't let anyone hurt me."

This was a backward child who wore coats on warm days and shorts on cool ones. A child who would rather eat flowers and roots than find friends to play with. A boy who would sing to himself about people understanding each other and having happiness and good health. And on this day, seeing him standing in the bees, braids swaying, without being touched harmfully at all, I realized my son had inherited a gross innocence about the world. I feared for him.

By the time a year had passed, Vaughan had entered bilingual Headstart after being identified as an ESL student. Travis was in first grade and rode in a therapeutic horse program (Heads-Up), which paired disabled people with horses and implemented occupational therapy while mounted. Travis really enjoyed this program, and his self-confidence was enhanced greatly by the horse he was paired with. Anyone who works with horses knows well the healing nature of their contact. The program worked so well that I dreamed of initiating similar programs in Indian communities throughout the United States and Canada. The benefits were obvious, and the spectrum of benefiters could include many disabilities: physical, emotional, and spiritual disabilities; early childhood to adult disabilities; disabilities involving veterans, victims of domestic violence, FAS victims, and a variety of other people of need. It would be a way to pair expert horsemen and horsewomen with health practitioners, educators, and children and other community people in need—a way to build community. I began immediately to share my dream with many of my close friends and work-related contacts, and we spent as much time in the program as they would allow.

Although both of my boys were receiving physical and occupational therapies, they demonstrated quick minds nonetheless, spending weekends painting watercolors and selling them curbside like other kids sold lemonade and cookies. Both boys started dancing, Vaughan drummed, and Travis began to act in some playhouse productions. It seemed that whatever interested me interested them too. We were close, sticking together and moving forward, growing happier and more peaceful in our own place.

My parents reentered my life, and I as a grown woman had to learn to be a mother to my own mother. My dad called, reporting that my brother was beating them up again and confessing that he didn't know how much more he could take. Because the elder abuse laws in California were decades ahead of those in the South, Pumpkin and I plotted to remove and relocate our parents to save their lives. We convinced my dad to put their house and property in North Carolina up for sale and begin making necessary repairs on their home. My mother wasn't informed of our plan, or of the sale, until prospective buyers were brought through, and luckily the house sold relatively quickly. My immediate family was left only with some mineral rights lease land left to us by Grandpa Vaughan on the Plains. It was an incredibly sad but necessary sacrifice for their survival.

My sister flew out to drive them across country. We knew my mother would never submit to coming along with me, but she liked Pumpkin, and if anyone could convince her she could. My part would be to keep them at my new place and help them find a home of their own before getting my mother back into the hospital for badly needed mental health care.

Up to the curb pulls the decade-old, '77 red Ford 150 pickup truck that my dad bought a year after I purchased my first new vehicle from our tobacco crop in the mid-1970s. The front of the truck sports a cattle guard, looking out of place in Santa Paula. I see them from my bedroom window—my sister, mother, and father, all dark headed and greasy faced from driving cross-country. My sister is the only one smiling, that particular smile with which one attempts to alter moods of those with less ability to perceive optimism. Pumpkin approaches the duplex with the speed of someone familiar with cities, my father ambling slowly behind her. I ask them in for coffee, encouraging them to make themselves at home in whichever room they wanted.

My mother sits in the pickup, facing forward, refusing to come in, insisting they return home. After her endless complaining about North Carolina for as far back as I could remember, suddenly it had become home to her too. No one can convince her that there is no "home" anymore. She stays in the truck for the next three days, coming in only to use the bathroom and to take some coffee in Styrofoam cups back to the truck.

At one point, she turns to me and barks, "I am not living with you. I hate you, and I've hated you since the day you were born." My mother has long been away from Canada, from her beloved Canadian Rockies, and the "eh"s and "aaayee"s are all but gone from her speech.

"Alright Mom," I answer, half-amused.

Pumpkin blurts out, "That's not very nice. You apologize to her right now."

It is strange to hear Pumpkin because she has never before this time defended me. My mother smiles, the smile of a child taunting another, and with the sarcasm mustered on playgrounds says, "Alright. IIII'mmmm sssssssooorr-rrry." She tilts her head this way and that, laughing off her own words, the hiss slipping across her dentures and driving the nerve endings on the back of my neck stiff. Suddenly my sister and I are Pumpkin Head and Baby No again, hiding our heads under pillows with transistors jammed to our ears and singing. I begin to sing out loud; in a couple of bars Pumpkin joins me.

On the fourth day Mom rises from the truck and walks through the front door. No surrender really—she is still peeved but needs to communicate her complaints to us in a different manner. She wants attention. My dad explains to her that there is no going back, the house and land are sold, and there is nothing to go back to. She agrees to stay for two weeks, insisting that if I can't find a place for them she is going back.

For the next ten days I drove my dad to every vacant place we could find in Santa Paula. The sale of his house and property had yielded around $30,000, enough (in California in the late 1980s before the inevitable real estate crash) to purchase a thirty-year-old mobile home in a seniors' park on rented trailer space. The main problem we confronted was racism. Liberal California is a myth manufactured for postcards and the tourist industry. In my opinion, there is no liberal state in America. Tolerance is the true myth. One seniors' park we visited apparently abided by an unwritten rule of whites only. When the real estate agent made an offer on the trailer for my parents, the park manager eyed the "Custer wore Arrow shirts" bumper sticker on my dad's truck, took a hard look at my dad and mom, and asked the agent if they were Indians. If so, he asserted, it would cause "problems" for the "quality" previously established in the park. This remark infuriated the real estate agent, who was a Urias, a prominent Mexican businessman. He threatened the seniors' park with a lawsuit, and we bought the trailer. Soon the park had a new manager, but the damage to my aging parents' self-esteem was already done.

My dad began to talk less openly about Indian ways or about anything important culturally. He now tried more consciously to blend in and adapt to his surroundings. Driven from home and beaten down by prejudice, by years of my mother's mental illness, and by his own son, he seemed to sacrifice his true strength — his pride in who he was — in order to cope with these new circumstances. He was at the end of solutions, and it appeared that his only choice was to accept and adapt. Witnessing this transformation was one of the saddest times of my life.

When my dad visited me now he spoke rarely of living and much of death. Pumpkin was politically active in San Francisco, and I continued being involved in fund-raisers and gatherings. Concerned for our safety after seeing Pumpkin at a rally on CNN, Dad would utter pronouncements like "I wish I hadn't have told you so much. Now the feds will have to kill you" or "We don't need any more martyrs. We've had enough already." Having already raised us with the responsibility of defending our people and our way of life, his newly developed concern, however, had little impact because we realized he was tired. He was in his late sixties and worn out from caring for our mother for over three decades of insanity. Pumpkin and I knew his life needed some peace for him to continue living.

We began planning to take conservatorship of our mother. Dehl, who had been in California for a long time, suggested a mental hospital, Vista Del Mar, for my mother's care. I drove out there and was amazed at the resort atmosphere, so far removed from the institutions she had been confined and shocked in. I called Pumpkin to come down, and we began court proceedings.

It would seem that, after thirty-some years of institutionalization for chronic mental illness, it wouldn't have been too difficult for my sister and I to gain conservatorship over our mother. Unexplained factors, however, always come into play when dealing with insanity—believe me—and the truly insane have uncanny abilities to convince seemingly normal people that nothing is wrong with them. My mother was educated at McGill and has a great ability to persuade due to her gift of articulation and lucid spells. By the time she was done interviewing with her public defender, he was convinced we were horrible people who only wanted to put her away somewhere. During the court proceedings, the public defender denied that anything had ever been wrong with her, began referring to our mother as eccentric rather than mentally ill, and insisted she have the right to do whatever she pleased under the state of California's elder protection codes since she was fast approaching seventy.

In the end, my mother proved again to be her own worst enemy. She wrote unsolicited letters to the judge claiming not only that my sister and I were controlled by governmental computer programmers but that he himself was "robotted" by the Buggers as well. After long and difficult hearings, the conservatorship was granted, and we were given joint guardianship over her health care, mental health care, and physical needs. The public defender fought and won her the right to retain control over her financial affairs.

The first matter of task for my mother's care was to obtain new glasses. The bottle-bottom thick lenses of her glasses were so badly scratched it was a wonder she could see through them at all. She had flatly refused new lenses since before World War II, claiming always that the eye doctor at McGill had approved the prescription and that they were just fine. I drove her to the optometrist's office in Ventura and had her eyes examined before helping her select a new pair. The eye doctor I chose was very understanding, coming out with us to look at the frames available. She was so childlike in the shop, wondering at the many possible selections, that I had to smile. Finally she decided I should pick a frame for her since she couldn't decide on her own. When I slipped the empty frames on her face, she turned to ask me how they looked, knocking over three stands of frames in the process. Not comprehending the ruckus, my mother stood there beaming, wondering what I thought of her new glasses.

I asked Pumpkin for help when I decided to commit Mom to Vista Del Mar, seeking a different medication for her illness (I discovered that she was covered by my dad's government insurance and Medicare, so it wouldn't cost a thing). I preregistered her and made an appointment to bring her in.

Now came the true test of our authority. Pumpkin and I were scarred by memories of her being taken away in straitjackets when we were young. Pumpkin didn't know if she could stand making her go; I knew we had no choice. We told Dad our plans and left him with my boys so he wouldn't have to deal with it. My sister and I drove over to our mother's home and announced our intentions in as gentle a way as possible. First she continued to lie on the living room couch, refusing to budge. I announced that we would have to carry her out if she wouldn't come voluntarily. Telling Pumpkin to grab her feet, I curled my arms under her upper body and lifted.

Pumpkin stood there staring at me, petrified, murmuring, "I can't."

I couldn't believe it. After the court process, the planning, and the selling of their place in North Carolina, now my sister wanted to back out. Hot and tired of waiting, I said I would take her myself and began pulling Mom off the couch. My mother began to fight, screaming and kicking and wringing away, and then locked herself in the bathroom. It seemed humorous to me, but Pumpkin was torn. Looking as though she might cry, my sister nonetheless raised her voice loud enough so our mother could hear her through the door, threatening to open it forcibly. I told my mom that she was forcing me to pick the lock and that we were taking her no matter what.

We had all learned to pick locks under my dad's guidance as small children. (The skill was useful if someone tried to kill themselves in the bathroom because my dad would most likely have been at work and our mother would have been either in an asylum or too busy with delusions to notice.) I straightened a wire coat hanger and began opening the lock by inserting the wire into the doorknob. Mom suddenly came barreling out the bathroom door, grabbing her purse and declaring that she would not be strong-armed by us "bad, BAD girls." She hurriedly walked out to the car and got in the back seat.

Pumpkin drove the car, and I rode in the back with my mother. Along the way she vacillated between branding us as "bad, bad girls, strong-arming me," to announcing, "I will report this," to commenting on the "pretty" street lights and stoplights that she called "Christmas lights." I laughed at her remarks, and Pumpkin become increasingly furious at me. I couldn't help it really. Humor was the only way I could ever deal with her behavior, and admittedly she came out with truly hysterical associative leaps in thought at times. My mother didn't notice my laughing and at one point expressed her happiness that we were all going for a ride together. I could not quit laughing.

Upon arriving at Vista Del Mar, Mom refused to budge, so they sent orderlies to come and get her and put her in lockdown. I explained to her that if she came in peacefully they would admit her into a personal room, but she was stubborn and ended up in lockdown at the back of the facility, where they observed patients for violence before releasing them into the population of in-hospital care. She was so angry, mostly with me, when we left that I didn't visit until she asked for me several days later. By then she was surprisingly thankful and said they treated her well and listened to everything she had to say. Perhaps she was so unfamiliar with anything else in California that the institution actually made her feel at home. A Dr. Thurston had been assigned to her and had prescribed Haldol. Some effects were almost immediate; others would come over years of monthly injections. The only thing she was unhappy about was taking the medication itself, which she insisted was part of a greater governmental plot and useless. At last, though, her shock treatment years and time without medication were finally over.

It was good having my mother more sedate. She still believed the delusions, but little by little they drove her less to hysteria. And, for the first time in our collective family memory, she even developed a sense of humor. My dad relaxed and began working on things around their trailer, and the boys benefited from their grandparents' company and example. My kids, my parents, and I finally settled into

Santa Paula and visited mostly with each other, Derya and Dehl, Sandy (a Registry worker from the Mt. Shasta area), and my boys' babysitter, Cheryl, all of whom I had grown to respect and appreciate as true friends. I easily grew tired of California, though, and would take off with the boys to stay with friends in South Dakota, Colorado, and the Southwest for several months out of each year. I guess I never really gave in to being a part of the California community, probably spending as much time out of the state as I did within.

My brother eventually showed up on a new Harley and moved in with my parents, taking over control of telephone calls and entries into their trailer as well as dictating shopping and other excursions. I complained about it to my boyfriend, Manuel, who responded, "Sounds like he needs his ass kicked." The next day the police came to our apartment to notify me that Manuel had done exactly that. The police wanted me to press charges, but all I could do was laugh at them. My brother had terrorized me for most of my life, physically hurting me more than anyone other than Tom. When he last called me from a Carolina jail, he referred to me as a welfare slut, said we made him hurt us, blamed his drug and alcohol abuse on my not telling him our mom was crazy, accused me of not raising him better (though we are only fifteen months apart), for, for not, for, for not . . . until I finally hung up the phone. I decided to ostracize him officially until he agreed to get psychological help and alcohol and chemical treatment. It is a vow I made to myself that exists even today and one I am sorry for because I still love him. I am also grateful for the vow because it has spared me so much pain and possibly loss of life. My father ostracized his brother Sam decades before, and I am my father's daughter, as life reminds me again and again.

I'll touch briefly here on Manuel, whom I eventually married for a short time. Manuel's mother was from Arizona (Indian and Spanish) and his dad was raised in Mexico (mestizo). He was a working man, doing concrete work in construction, was strong, and could do many things on his own. It was familiar and attractive to me. As for him, I overheard him once bragging to a friend that his Mexican coworkers thought I was white (prestigious at that time for them) because I was so light, and his family was pleased because I was a mixed-blood who believed in traditional ways. We got married when he came back from the army.

Manuel's main problem was that he was jealous of me. He didn't like my attending Pow Wows and gatherings—my older boy had just begun to dance, the younger enjoyed sitting in on drum, and I, not knowing many people here, enjoyed cooking bread, working the booths with my girlfriends, and tabulating for the contests. He was jealous of most of the doings we went to and always accused me of snagging. Some of my girlfriends tried to talk to him, to assure him that his suspicions were ungrounded, to try to involve him somehow in what we were doing already, but it did little good.

Even though Manuel gave me a hard time, he was good with my kids. His people were into family, and since he had no kids of his own he spent a lot of time with my boys doing "guy things." Vaughan completely accepted him, both called him Dad, and his nieces and nephews claimed the boys for cousins. His parents treated all of us as though we had always been part of their family, and they treated each other well. Sitting in their house, in a house with furniture from good stores and newer appliances, in a house with a large-screen television in color, I thought, *this must be what normal is.* His mother even taught me to use the dishwasher in our apartment and to make salsa, guacamole, and turkey tamales with masa.

Our marriage was soon over. When I was diagnosed with a new malignancy, he bought a twelve pack, dropped me off at the apartment, and left—it was *my* problem. I didn't see him for about three weeks, until after the treatment was all done with. Later I went off to a gathering with my kids and came home to find him on crank (he'd begun using with his reserve unit). Walking in, I found all my clothes ripped up and my family's pictures shattered in the frames and stacked up on the bed. One was a photograph of him and my youngest son; he had not only broken the glass but torn the picture in two so that they were separated physically. While I was looking at this photograph and wondering what was going on with him, Manuel was hiding behind the door. When I turned he smashed me facedown into the glass and held me there for a few minutes before lifting me from my feet and throwing me across the room into a wall. I got up, got the kids, and left out their bedroom window; when he was gone, I returned, changed the locks, packed up all his things, and then visited with his mother and father and told them I was moving him out. They gave their approval, and I put the boxes in a rental storage unit under his name.

A few days after I moved him out, Manuel called drunk from a pay phone, claiming he had a gun and was going to kill himself if I didn't take him back. I called the cops and got the kids ready about the time he appeared at our locked front door. I told him to stand in front of the window and take off his shirt so I could see for myself if he was packing. I could see no weapon (the gun, it turns out, was in his truck), and I was just going to go out and see what he wanted when the cops arrived and took him into custody. Luckily, I was able to get the marriage certificate annulled. It was not a divorce, not a failure, but something that just happened.

We returned to South Dakota to stay with friends for a time. Up north the boys and I were pretty happy. Men would bring by deer they had downed and I'd butcher them, so we shared the kill and provided for other people. Once they came late at night and woke me, with three bucks downed and pickup lights to skin by. Getting up, I went to work on them right away. It was so dark I was using a machete to quarter instead of cutting everything up, just to get it sized down enough to put away.

Working on the third deer, my hand was under the skin and around a hindquarter, and it felt strange, spongy. I called someone to pull the truck closer so I could see but couldn't get a good sight on it in the night. At sunup the gangrene was obvious. I remembered my own gangrene, at age seven from tonsillitis, ignored for too long. I pitied the deer for carrying the illness and was glad they downed him to prevent further suffering. I knew we should bury the meat to keep other animals from getting to it. Due to a severe drought that year, it would be difficult, though, to bury a whole deer in the sun-baked earth.

A twelve-year-old boy named Stacy offered to get his grandpa Ernie's car to carry off the carcass. We tied it by rope across the trunk and headed out over the hills off the road. The car was bumping pretty hard on the rock-solid ground, and the deer came off twice before we got to an old wash to lay it down. We headed back up to Highway 50 and loaded the trunk with road gravel stacked by the side of the road for construction crews. Covering the deer with gravel, we prayed and then headed back.

We had no running water at the time and usually went to Springfield to fill jugs and swim in the Missouri River every couple of days. Because it was early morning after we had buried the deer and were ready to clean up quickly, we went to a gas station in front of the Avon Motor Court to use their bathrooms and hose. A handful of farmers getting coffee and gas froze as Stacy and I walked in, completely covered with dried blood from pulling the skinned carcass around. The farmers looked at us like we were ghosts. Realizing we must have looked like the perpetrators of a chainsaw massacre, we busted up laughing and couldn't quit until we reached home.

While shuttling back and forth between California and the Plains, I was offered an opportunity to serve as a board member for the American Indian Registry for Performing Arts. I accepted. After a short time on the board, the chairman suggested I take over a directorial position on the staff and the board approved it. Although most of my pay would be contingent upon securing grants, I quit school (since my greater reasons for attending the workshop were being realized in the new position), left two paid part-time jobs, and took a hiatus from teaching workshops. A close working friend, Wesley Black Elk, joined me as my boss in the Registry office. I'd worked with Wes writing grants for North Star (his own organization supporting dancers and artists) and knew he was competent, easy to work with, dependable, and trustworthy in hard times.

We worked hard writing grants, establishing plans for new programs, and trying desperately to gain funding for the organization, which had lost its entire financial support previous to our administration. Our second major goal was to ensure that all of the membership had referrals to auditions and opportunities to become employed. I think we worked around eleven to twelve hours a day regularly for eight months, though I do remember working for twenty hours straight many times due to approaching deadlines during the initial grant-writing phase. During the first eight months we worked without funding or pay, our hours to be paid later when the grants we wrote together were approved. We could not receive help from social services (food stamps, housing, and so on) to tide us over, and (not wanting to live in a city even if I did have to work in one) I had to commute ninety miles to Los Angeles each direction daily, so transportation alone was a nightmare. My own father repaired our office equipment and donated our petty cash several times just to keep us afloat.

At that time we were also lobbying intensely for Indians to play Indian roles in the performing arts. We made a good team—Wes was knowledgeable and quite conversant with upper-class crowds, and I wrote grants well and was extremely dedicated and verbal when defending others. I was so modest, protective of my family, and publicity shy that I switched my first and middle names and used them as an alias to do the work (something I'd done when protesting, organizing, performing, and songwriting because I really didn't want the personal attention). I can explain that decision best by borrowing a good phrase: "I wanted to do important things, but I never wanted to be important."

We were a good team, but one confronting many challenges. Most of the administrative staff at the Registry had lived in California for years and at times criticized Wes and I for "acting like we just left the res." *So what?* we thought. True, we weren't cultured in metropolitan ways, but Wes and I had both been farmed out as kids and had traveled quite a bit. In turn, I admit, we sometimes believed the staff to be spiritually depleted and culturally crippled from urban life, and we thought it our duty to help them out. Regardless, we were dedicated to getting the job done even in extreme circumstances—I completed one proposal while hospitalized for toxic shock syndrome, complete with fevers and hallucinations—for the sake of the membership and for our firm belief in the late founder Will Sampson's dream of change for the benefit of the future of Indian people in the entertainment industry. Wes, Dehl, Ernie Fragua Whitecloud, Grant Britton, Nick Ramus, a couple of strong Screen Actors' Guild Indian lobbyists/representatives—Carol Marie and Jim Elk (coincidentally both Tsa la gi)—and many general members gave never-ending support and gratitude. We congratulated each other for reestablishing funding for the organization in Will's memory.

The Registry position enabled us to help people daily. When Indian actors or performers were treated unfairly, we made as many calls as it took to rectify the situation. When Native people came into town in two-hundred-dollar cars, just as we had, we put them up on the office couch, referred them to legitimate acting schools, and told them where to get motel vouchers and food, while calling producers to make sure their auditions were scheduled as planned. We had several major projects in the making and were referring as many performers as we could for auditions and technical work. When the Porcupine Singers called because they were having problems in Rapid City with the *Dances with Wolves* project, we spent an entire afternoon doing what we could to let the producers and set crew know that it was not acceptable to mistreat Indian people in any way, on any location.

We worked ourselves hard, firmly committed to implementing growth and representing the membership to the best of our abilities. In addition to calling the first general membership meeting of the organization, Wes and I were committed to the idea of ensuring that each and every Registry member was referred to an audition every quarter of the year and would be polled for their input on Registry services. We began recruiting new members and received pledges from many fine, established actors to teach and provide workshops during the upcoming grant period. We moved the Registry office from a hard-to-find back-street location to an office located in the former American Federation of Radio and Television Artists building on Hollywood Boulevard, just down from the Chinese Mann Theater. We began organizing and planning formal benefits and implementing changes even though we weren't receiving our pay.

I guess both of our childhoods had prepared us for such challenges and sacrifice. It was not unusual to our natures to be dedicated and devoted to something we believed in firmly. We wanted to help our people and to realize the dream of Indian people to portray themselves and tell their own story.

Months later, when the grants were finally approved and before the funding actually came in, we took our first actual weekend break. Wes and I went to a gathering together, where he was to meet up with his girlfriend and where I somehow encountered his cousin Al. It wasn't the first time we'd met, but this time it affected me differently.

I have a certain gift, and to this day I am plagued by it—the ability simply to look deeply at someone and instantly care, to wipe out any past they may have had and look at them for this moment in time. Maybe because I'd seen so much at so young an age, nothing looked bad to me if I could see the good. Maybe because I was able to make myself appear uncaring when I felt as though at times I was nothing but heart. Maybe because I have had so many people sit in judgment of me, I flat refuse to hold that position with any other. Maybe Mole gets bored and begins to look for something to do and watches single women, and maybe he sometimes makes bargains with the spirits of men who need someone to walk with, and maybe he sneaks out at night and captures my heart and lets them possess it for a while, and maybe the man himself doesn't know his spirit is making this bargain so he doesn't know what to do with me once he has me going. Maybe Mole is always bargaining. I don't know. Regardless of the origin of my feelings at the time, the affection was in motion and I was swept away.

When Al first approached me, I was cooking fried potatoes in a screen tent. Coming up behind me and admiring the pan, he asked if I was cooking for him. When I handed him a plate, he asked me if I'd marry him right then and there. I laughed, but he looked me right in the eye and said, "I'm serious, I'm sick. I need somebody just like you." Later that day he jumped out of his family's pickup and pumped gas into my car in town, thoroughly washing down all the windshields, then refusing to let me pay for my own gas and convenience store food, saying, "Let's go somewhere beautiful, move far away from people, and stay together."

I was struck by his efforts and thought he was a fine-looking man. Long black hair, dark brown eyes, pure Indian face and build, six foot two. I knew he had lots of girlfriends, and even at this gathering many women were tailing him. But this time something was different, and

I knew from the moment he walked in the tent I'd already started falling for him.

I needed time. I've always been enormously open-hearted — no doubt about it — but I didn't know enough about Al to gauge whether he could hang. I needed a man with a strong heart and a sense of loyalty or no man at all. Fairly traumatized by abuse and by the carcinoma, I stayed shy of Al for some time, encouraging him to do what he always did and agreeing to see him sometimes. I reminded him that there were lots of women around, but I also told him I wasn't out to tie anyone down (*how could I promise that to anyone, walking with carcinoma anyway?*). I wanted time to see for myself what he was about.

Inside, I wanted to settle down someplace, reorchestrate my life, and find absolute peace, but I had become that mare who'd been beaten too many times, that horse spooked from sudden movements near the eyes, the one jumping away from, rather than following along, a path with too many tangled roots. I knew what I wanted, but I couldn't take the easy way through. I simply didn't know how to go about it.

For a while, because I was so shy and would only look for him if I had something to say, he got the impression (as I learned later) that I wasn't really attracted to him, and he really believed I wasn't interested in having a relationship. I'd learned early on that sometimes just not saying anything at all, when so much needed to be said, was a better method of defense. Hence the shyness. Remaining reserved enough to observe before falling too deep into something too big to climb back out of. Pushing someone away before they could see into my gentle side.

Al continued visiting with lots of other women and going about his life, but he always kept tabs on me. Regardless of my misleading impression, he asked me to marry him every day we talked, sometimes twenty times a day (even more later on). He'd call and check on making arrangements here and there from pay phones, with me standing next to him, sometimes handing me the phone to ask questions. He always said he knew what he wanted and that he couldn't wait. I figured if he asked me that many times he must be used to asking lots of women — probably still was — so I never could take his proposals seriously. I figured that as long as he had company he would be okeh and I could care from a distance and pray for him and things would still be good that way.

I admit freely today that I regret being so afraid of men after my previous experiences that I literally couldn't answer his serious questions about feelings. I couldn't even respond. He'd ask and I'd turn my head, let my hair fall to cover my face, change the subject, or sometimes just look at him. It's not that I didn't want to. I just couldn't make the words come out. It's like they were caught somewhere deep inside me, and I didn't have the knowledge to understand how to make them come out. My past was too painful to describe, too hard to articulate coherently, too much to give Al because it seemed to hurt him to know how I had been hurt before.

Given time, I am able to show what I do not have words for; luckily I had time for this man to know the truth. Nonetheless, it was difficult for us to begin the relationship at all because he needed words when I needed silence; he needed to hear things I could only demonstrate. I am grateful he was patient and continued pursuing me without pressuring me, because if it had been solely up to me I probably would have let him believe whatever he wanted and maybe would have checked in every year or two, when time had allowed purer understanding, checked to make sure he was all right, that he had someone to care for him, to take care of him and maybe eventually would have let him know I cared without asking for anything in return, would have gone peacefully back on my way.

Not surprisingly, Al became obviously frustrated with me until he admitted he had progressing leukemia, thus allowing me the opportunity to reveal my own slow-growing carcinoma. At that point he understood my fear of perhaps not having enough quality future to give anyone to make a firm commitment and my fear of having the sickness turned against me when I did fall ill again, and I was fairly sure I would. Negative searches out positive, and positive is all I held for my home, my children, and for this man.

Over the next couple of months Al and I talked on the phone. He was in Denver. I was in the process of relocating to an area in the northern part of Los Angeles County, closer to where Travis rode in Heads-Up and to my workplace, an area with progressive Little

League and soccer teams for Vaughan. Busy with my kids and with packing and unpacking, I was working, working, working. When we saw each other in person again, we walked together from that day on.

It was good—no accusations, no questioning, no games, no pressuring, none of that mind-game controlling stuff that made me shut down and get quiet and put up with things I never should. He became completely sincere and kind toward me. In this relationship this time, I was completely floored by the amount of respect this man showed me. It was as if he could see through all my guardedness, accept it, then allow me to come to terms with him in my own time. The relationship we created was easy. It was him and me, and we were all happy and things were good. Sometimes, in the joint refusal to have anything bad between us, we seemed to grow to the same mind and heart. It may sound simplistic, but living it was amazing really. This was the first time in my life I felt free to try to show my true self, my extremely gentle and affectionate ways of being and perceiving the world.

But that was before anyone else found out about us. Once other people knew, we had to defend each other. Wes was pretty worried and scolded me; I told him it was between Al and me and shouldn't concern him. Wes later told me that Al called him and told him in Indian that what we did was nobody's business but our own and what was between us was just that. He told him that he was tired of taking care of himself and was happy with what we had worked out and that it was going to be this way. Al's sister told me not to worry, that people would accept it eventually because we were living together anyway.

I never understood why Wes thought his cousin was going to hurt me—maybe because he'd seen me walk through my last relationship and knew about my kids' dad, maybe because we had been friends for years and he knew my weaknesses, or maybe because both Al and I had pasts. But Wes needn't have worried. His cousin was good to me, and I was committed to him.

Now that I was with someone who could go the mile, he was sickened by leukemia. I had lived with cancer for a few years already, surgery after surgery, too many biopsies to keep up with. But leukemia doesn't give you the time of squamous cell. It's an unforgiving cancer, progressing rapidly. Al's time was approaching no matter what we wanted.

I'd already been through so much I knew I could hang through it, but I just didn't want to see him go. This was the first time in my life I tried to allow anybody to know me truly, the first time I had ever even begun to open up to a man. This was the first and only time anyone had ever witnessed my true nature as a woman, walking in a half-side relationship. He was so patient with me. We never had bad words or thoughts. Normal differences of opinion would emerge, as for anyone, but we worked to understand each other's perspective when it happened and often came to a mutual understanding. And we stood together. I began to believe we would find peace and placement together.

As far as my boys went, he devoted time and affection to them as if they were his own and cried to me many times over his three boys, whom he had lost custody of and didn't see much anymore. This was the most vulnerable area of loss, I think, in his life, and he talked of them often.

By fall Al was hospitalized in Denver. I was up in South Dakota and Colorado, on unpaid Registry business, checking the *Dances with Wolves* set in Pierre, looking into possible Tribal Film Commission sites, and visiting friends and claimed relations. I came down and stayed with him and never left, putting in ahead of time for a leave of absence at work (by then Nick Ramus had taken over as chairman of the board and had given me a written leave). My kids stayed at my dad's, and I remained at the hospital with Al until he was released.

Though I wished we could go on forever, I knew in my heart I was looking at walking him through his death. To me it was an honor to be able to do this for him. Death is a natural thing and, as I have mentioned, something my dad raised us to never fear. So I never even considered my being with him in those final days a hardship or never thought about avoiding it in any way. It is true, though, that also in my heart I secretly believed in a chance of his survival, which is what I prayed for and what I spoke of. I did understand on a spiritual and emotional level that what we were experiencing was probably the purest form of human exchange in life, save the birth of children, and I was thankful for the welcome break from chaos.

All through that time of sickness I was sincerely happy too. Al accepted me, wanted to know me, and cared for me without condition. I cannot remember one time after we began to keep company with each other when he ever criticized me or offended me in any way. He defended me even to my own relatives. No one could say anything about me or bad to me when he was alive. For the first time in my life, I found that when I could share openly there was no denial on his part of the fact that I had lived my own life. Having such trust and acceptance gave me the right to relax and proved to me that love means "without hurt." It was a momentous blessing.

I never could talk about my feelings for him though. I wanted to, but I was so used to feelings being dangerous that I couldn't bring myself to verbalize them. We never had time. But he was so understanding he'd say I didn't need to tell him because I showed him my feelings every day and that meant much more than saying it aloud. He said he knew people had hurt me and that he never wanted me to feel that again from him or anybody else. He said I deserved more, that I was a good Indian woman with a big heart and all anyone needed to walk with and be happy with if they'd take the time to know me. He appreciated me and made me feel I was a worthwhile human being.

In the hospital, Al agreed to try chemotherapy. His hair, that long, dark, beautiful hair, fell out in massive clumps, and his body withered with weight loss. He was obviously in extreme pain and requested some medication to ease things. The nurses refused to give him anything one night because they insisted he was an addict, judging from the bruises up and down his arm that were in fact merely residuals from blood draws and tests. Furious, though I never let him see me upset, I demanded to see the chief of staff on call and insisted that they give him something for pain right away. After hearing me out, he agreed that medication was in order and said that even if he was an addict he deserved alleviation.

On good days in the hospital, days when the pain was tolerable and he could be taken on walks in a wheelchair or later by using a walker, he would wrap his head in a bandanna to prevent his baldness from showing. When we returned to the room I would reach over and take it off, saying he didn't need to hide from me and that he was still a handsome man, haired or not. Glancing in the mirror, Al would look at me and shake his head and smile, but as soon as anyone else came into the room he replaced the bandanna.

When old girlfriends stopped by to visit, I would use the opportunity to get some coffee or wash up. My leaving really bothered him, and Al would beg me not to leave him alone with particular women.

"Don't you ever get jealous?" or "Don't you have a jealous bone in your body?" he'd ask.

"It's none of my business," I'd reply. "I *trust* you. Why would I worry when I have trust with you? You could probably make me jealous, but you don't. Maybe they need this time to settle old issues with you. It's not going to hurt anything if old issues are resolved and people can go on in their lives without carrying them. You never put anyone ahead of me. Never hurt me. Don't worry about it."

One woman had a child with her who certainly looked like him, and I pitied her. I am a woman too. And no matter how much I cared for him, there was nothing he could have said to convince me not to leave the room then.

One night I woke with him singing to me and stroking my face, which was not uncommon, but a heart machine was being wheeled into the room and electrodes were hooked up to his chest. He probably had had a heart attack. Here he was stroking my forehead and cheeks with the back of his hand and singing for me, and I began to plead with him to forget about me and rest himself.

"I am," he said. "You're always taking care of me and looking after me. You're a strong woman, you never ask for much, but I need to take care of you too. I want to."

I didn't feel strong, but I never spoke this. It was as if speaking weak words would only make one or both of us weaker. So like that willow in a bad wind, I kept my courage up and nodded my head.

After Al was released, he gradually began walking without aid and grew stronger. For a while I think he had faith in the chemo, while I tended to believe in his spiritual strength. Never once did I cry openly, out of respect for him holding his own, but when we prayed we both let tears fall. Through the night he would hold onto me, not hanging on, not clinging to me, but like he was protecting me from the world, slowly beginning to accept he was going to go and leave me here on my own. He would hold me like this for hours and talk to me, slowly but almost nonstop, until everything he could possibly think of to share was with me somehow. I have been told he was a quiet, reserved man, but I cannot attest to this because he was full of words while he was with me, sharing constantly his philosophies, feelings, beliefs, stories, songs, and prayers. Al confided his dreams of "taking off" with me and finding someplace "far away from other houses, people, where we could settle down and live good, with love, and prayer, surrounded by beauty and quiet peaceful country." He said he had a dream of creating a children's center and a traditional mortuary at Wounded Knee for people who didn't believe in being embalmed. I confessed I wanted to initiate Heads-Up programs in Indian Country and create mediation and advocacy centers and refuges where youth and women leaving abusive situations could use art and writing as a vehicle of transcendence. Language centers. Community dreams. He'd share for hours, then ask me my own—and listen. Encouraging me to follow my dreams, accepting, giving nonstop appreciation, more than I'd known anyone to give at that time.

The last time he was in Denver University Hospital, the doctors called me into the hall and told me he probably had six weeks to live. I heard them, knowing it could happen that way, but I didn't want to hear them, so I prayed and ignored the time measurement completely. I could not have borne a countdown, such a white way of thinking. I never mentioned it until he straight up asked over six weeks later. I couldn't lie to him. When he heard their exact words, Al began staying up all night almost every night talking to me, singing, giving me his utmost attention, sharing what he knew and didn't know, and asking my opinion or perspective of things as if he didn't want to waste a moment of living on sleep. I would have to talk him into sleeping through the mornings and taking naps to maintain his level of strength. To some extent this was already true, but from that day on every moment was devoted to total communication, affection, song, story, good thoughts, and constant prayer.

I'd been in Denver for over a month already when Al asked to go with me to California. He'd been there a few times and liked it; being away from everybody you knew also had its advantages. So we went to my home in Canyon Country together, on the way stopping in Vegas. Al tried very hard to talk me into marrying him right then and there. If we did, his family would misrepresent the bond, so I said we should wait. He answered that he didn't know how long we could do that, it was what he wanted, and he didn't care about anybody else. I wanted to marry him, but I was scared. We drove on.

In California he seemed healthier and happier immediately. Seeming to enjoy life, Al spoke often about wanting to live now that he "had something." "Stick with me through this," he would ask over and over. "Just stick with me." Other times he would say, "Take me with you wherever you go, even after I leave, take me with you, find a place we'd be happy and settle there, with your kids, take my land—I want you to have it, no one can say anything, just move there and settle in with your kids, and if mine need a place to stay later keep them for me. Put up a children's center, a traditional mortuary, relax, do what you want—live in peace, write your heart out—help people that way—these are my wishes." Or sometimes he'd say, "Follow me when I go," though he would soon add in that I should wait until my kids are older. Both boys idolized him and soon were wrapping their heads in bandannas and drumming more and more. Sometimes Vaughan would sleepwalk at night, and Al would bring him in to lie near us until he was peaceful again. And always he would hold me protectively, singing, and always he had good words and stories for my boys.

I wished and prayed for him to live and never gave up hope. I wanted to believe we could have this life.

Inevitably he got sick again, and we took him to the City of Hope, a well-known cancer institute, on advice from a friend of his. "City of Hopeless" he called it upon touring the halls of the terminally ill he would now join. Here they drained all the blood from his body, circulating it through a machine adding plasma and white blood cells. Al was so weak I had to spoon-feed him; his only complaint was that I had to deal with it. He asked over and over how I could stand it, how I could stand him in this shape, how I could care for him through all of this, and I'd reassure him, saying it was nothing.

He kept his dignity through everything, and so did I.

The hospitals were always cold, and we were staying up all night, visiting and holding each other. I was shaking from the chill one December night when he asked, "Go get my jacket, okeh?" I went over to the closet, pulling out the blue Pendleton coat with a small star-blanket center star on the back sewn by a grandma.

When I brought it to him he said, "Keep it. You're always cold, just have it."

Even though the coat really comforted and warmed me, his words scared me.

One morning I was called away from his side to my boys' rural Mint Canyon School north of Canyon Country, because a fight had broken out. I was told in no uncertain terms that my kids had to be picked up immediately, and it would have taken hours for my dad to come from Santa Paula to take care of them. At this time Travis was in fourth grade and Vaughan in second, too young to be on their own alone.

I told Al I had to leave for a couple of hours, and he didn't want me to go. I didn't either. He never was happy when I had to leave his side, at home, at the hospital, in public. He would always say, "When you go, every ten minutes feels like a hundred years to me. Hurry back. The wait makes it hard." And I would feel nothing but guilt until I could see for myself that he was okeh when I returned.

I called from the road two hours later and told him I was on the way back. All he said was, "Hurry. I miss you. The only regret I have for this sickness and me going is having to leave you behind after I finally found something I always wanted in my life. Now, I want to live but it's too late."

When I returned to the hospital, bringing him some of his favorite snacks and tapes, Al was sleeping strangely. His face was never this way, and I was immediately concerned. Attempting to wake him, I called in nurses and asked what happened. Although they assured me everything was all right, I knew better.

Al awoke and told me how much he cared and wanted to be with me, wishing we could go on being happy. He then murmured that we were going somewhere else where nothing would bother us anymore. He asked me to kiss him and then closed his eyes. I knew what I didn't want to know, and my physical body realized how hard it was for me to let him go. It pained me so I could barely breathe on my own, and he began drumming on his chest in a heartbeat rhythm. Al was going into a coma, and they were wheeling him to have an MRI.

I took hold of his hand and said, "I care for you." I wanted to say more but didn't know how. I had no words. I didn't have the ability to formulate words into expressing how I really felt, and my eyes wanted to well. I had never let him see my tears all this time, and now, if I continued speaking, I knew they would flow, so I quickly touched his face without ever being able to say anything more.

Opening his eyes, he smiled and held onto my hand until he went unconscious. I knew he believed I loved him, and I knew he had no control over staying awake, and I think I held his hand for the next twelve hours straight, during tests and probes, following his stretcher down halls and floors and through an onslaught of leukemia experts milling about his bed in ICU.

That night the staff admitted they had overdosed him accidentally with the same medication four times in an hour. I was numb. I had stayed with him around the clock, and the one time I had to leave for my kids' sake they had overdosed him. It was unbelievable.

Two of his family members arrived and hurriedly decided to have his oxygen mask removed and let him go the next day. I was against it, believing that if it was his time he would pass, even with the nasal oxygen. I believed in giving him four days before final decisions were entertained, but they had legal right. I was unimportant in their decision; it was totally in their hands. Completely exhausted and thoroughly heartbroken, I prayed for him. Sang for him. Prayed. Saw him standing before me at the same time he lay physically on the bed. Saw him smile at me. I was still wearing his coat when I left ICU, and his scent was in the material. I buried my face into its collar and refused to feel bad for myself so I wouldn't affect him passing.

It was December 9, 1989.

I called my boys on the phone and told them he was gone. Travis was ecstatic that he wouldn't have to suffer anymore and that he would truly be "home" and free. They both made gifts and offerings for him and were young enough to understand that this is where we are all liberated without being old enough to have hang-ups about their own loss. In their innocence, I learned how I would conduct myself day to day for the next year.

White friends of his family were sent to our home and began to remove everything of his and the things we owned together. He had left me two checks to pay on our rent, and they demanded those also. They even stripped the coat he gave me off my back. I was completely unprepared. It was shocking, humiliating, and disgraceful.

After the funeral, Wes presented me with ribbons he'd worn as his cousin's pallbearer. Still pretty much in shock at the time, I was unable to drive or travel alone without experiencing short-term amnesia from the weight of the loss. Wes thanked me, recounting good words his cousin had said about my making him happy while he was living. Wes then hugged me and reminded me that no one could ever take away the truth—he knew we had found what so many people spend a whole life looking for and never stumble upon. I knew at that moment someone else accepted and understood, someone who missed him as much as I did, that Wes knew in his heart I had loved his relative to the best of my ability and without any regret for this time other than my own lack of verbal ability, and that we had to go on and be strong. Wes then personally asked me to write about my life and about this, about my relationship with his cousin and his death, and maybe about his own current relationship and our friendship—when I thought it was an appropriate time. Though I never said anything about it, I am indebted to Wesley always for this gift of hope and courage.

I am so very thankful for this time in my life. Thankful that I had been mostly sober for over ten years already so that I could see clearly and have a clear understanding of the process I was faced with and the clear capability of accepting its challenge of sacrifice, compassion, patience, and endurance without thinking about myself. I am thankful for this maturity, for the knowledge, for the many gifts I received in my life from this personal exchange, and I know in my heart that nothing can take that away, and the experience gives me the ability to have a more philosophical reasoning to this day. I thank Creator for this great test of my spirit and trust in my faith. For his company and faith in me. For this spiritual exchange in my life.

I was wounded and needed to move, far away from the City of Hope, far from our apartment. I suddenly realized I couldn't tolerate California any longer. I was so terribly furious at white people for their diseases, medicines, and all their crimes; I was so angry I couldn't even stand to listen to the radio because the music was all whitened somehow, and I wanted out. Months passed without a comprehensive indication of time. I couldn't handle the drapes opened and wanted it to be pitch black even in the midday.

I wasn't talking much about the event, but people became concerned about me. Al's adopted brother came to visit, expressing worry over us, insisting on paying rent and buying groceries. My mom and dad came by, and my mother exclaimed that she thought I had broken down. Taking me in the bedroom, she confided how she felt when her first husband was shot down in World War II, how she had mourned for him until she met my dad. When my friend Sandy and her family came by, they said I looked like a ghost; she feared for me, mourning so hard. Derya, already a sister to me, tried to keep me busy helping with her show in the main gallery at CalArts. The boys sat up and told me great stories and wrote songs for me. Dehl asked me and the kids to keep his house while he was in Mexico, just to get us out of the apartment. I enjoyed being out in his country place and ached for more simple surroundings myself. I needed to find this quiet place I had promised to settle in, the peace of mind we so truly desired in our lives. I wanted this for Al, in honor of him, and I needed it for myself and for my kids. We deserved it.

Three of my paternal uncles — John, Sid, and Sam — passed on very close together. I began to feel like I was being left behind.

The Registry was going through changes; overnight the entire staff was replaced (something I heard about secondhand, apparently on a supposition that money was missing although it hadn't even been issued from Washington yet or some other "jump-the-gun zealousness." I don't really know because I had been on leave for several weeks, was oftentimes still carrying out Registry work even so, but wasn't really involved with any of the issues). Wrestling with life and death issues and a great loss, I felt that if this action was the thanks we would receive for months of personal sacrifice solely for the benefit of the organization and its membership then the Registry would have to move ahead into a new era or would eventually be replaced with a stronger, more culturally sensitive organization. I'd already accomplished all I felt I needed to in that position. And other than clearing up some serious back pay issues, why should I suddenly begin to respond to false accusations and reactionary behavior at such a sobering time of understanding in life?

My close friend Diane Zephier, an Oglala attorney and community organizer, had just moved to Rapid City from Denver, herself mourning the loss of her youngest daughter to a brief, unexplained illness. She came out to California and convinced me to move there too, promising we would have nearby like company. I had no job, we didn't need the hospital or anything else here anymore, and my mother was responding well to her medication, so nothing personal was holding me here.

I knew nothing else to do but follow Al, and he was somewhere not ready for the likes of me, so taking his memory with me and physically following his body—which eventually was buried at the Wounded Knee Community Cemetery—I and my boys packed back up and moved up on a high hill, in the first round of the Black Hills, just west of Rapid City. That hill—where out the back we could see across the Black Hills clear to Harney Peak; where in front we could see clear to the Plains Badlands; where all sides sloped down and away from us and we felt as if we were in nests of the heavens; where the beauty rivaled lands more familiar to me, like the bluer-black Appalachian hills and thick green grass and woods full of deer and birds back home; where we had stopped many times on the way to Canada and spent time with our Dad when we were small; where we could look out and see beauty in all directions; where three eagles and seven deer crossed the path ahead of us as we walked around the house for the first time. Here, in this peaceful South Dakota quiet, the three of us, me and my two boys, found peace together.

The house was in fairly good shape, save for some broken windows and bullet holes that previous tenants from the biker free-for-all, the famous Sturgis Biker Rally, left in the shower wall. Two and a half acres of wooded hillside surrounded our home, and a cliff banked the west side. Sitting on the rock ledge, I could look out over the vast hills. The dirt drive, where deer and rabbit ambled alongside leading up the hill, sloped upward directly to the house, making it impossible to arrive at the house undetected. It felt truly safe. A porch on the front was large enough to sleep and stargaze on at night with the boys. That hill was like a great rock we could lean upon, where we found our own willow-like resilience with true tranquility. We loved it.

We were in fairly good shape too, mourning deeply, not unscathed, but whole. It felt as if we were starting over. Truly. An enormous evolution had occurred, coincidentally freeing us from our past, and nothing would ever be the same again. We were sound and felt it. Happy even more so. We felt a unity, a togetherness, unrivaled in my life for many years. My parents were safe in Santa Paula; my mom was in decent medical care. My sister was in a good place, with steady work, in San Francisco. My brother back in North Carolina was the only obvious casualty of the family at this point, ostracized for the safety of the whole, and we mourned him as if he were lost as well. The boys and I felt blessed and gave thanks, often and daily. We believed we were watched over, by our ghost ancestors, by our grandmas, grandpas, my auntie, uncles, cousins, and other relations, and by Al. That awareness stilled us and created a new motion for our little family to revel in: renewal.

We had a ten-year-old Audi that made it halfway through the first winter there, plus a well with good water and an industrial-sized coal furnace with a full-sized bin and auger. I had to climb into the bin to shovel coal into a mound for the auger to churn it to dust, and the furnace had to be piped clean and emptied once a week or so. This furnace kept the house warm on even the coldest South Dakota nights as long as the coal held a mound. If it dipped down into a funnel around the auger you'd have to get up, no matter what time of night, and shovel, so it kept me busy too. Though I wore a paper mask while shoveling, the dust continued coming out of my lungs for maybe six months after I quit shoveling for the season.

When it was warm, in the summer of 1990, my prayers for the truth to be known were answered, and I received a letter and check from the California Labor Board, who found that there was no wrongdoing on the part of our administration of the Registry, that I was wrongfully terminated during my leave of absence, and that the "true and essential facts of the case" were in my favor. The back wages I had worked for and earned from my position there had been awarded. It was a windfall of justice that allowed me time to live without worry of support for the three of us and enabled me to put the attempted personal injury far from my mind and our lives. Belief in time revealing truth proved right. Truth showed itself even though I refused to answer to unsubstantiated gossip and personal affronts. My dad's daughter through and through.

The next fall my boys began school at Horace Mann Elementary down in Rapid City. The boys were in third and fifth grades and immediately fit in better there than in the last three schools they'd attended. We mostly kept to ourselves and stayed home, but on occasion we would visit friends around the state. I managed to keep myself from too much social contact, though I did teach some art and writing workshops. That winter I went to work for GM, got a great employee discount, and ended up with the second new vehicle I would ever own in my life so I could drive the boys back and forth to school on blizzarding snow-covered roads and ice. A big, shaggy dog took up with us, showing up one day and unable to be chased away. We adopted him and accepted him as a good omen and company for the boys and for me.

When my boys came home from school, they would often pray outside before beginning to play, pick wild turnips, help till my small garden, or do chores. They were good boys. We openly loved each other and enjoyed life, and I could accept things while we remained there. I rarely left without reason. I was healing yet. Always, I would come home to the hill, look out across the treetops, watch the many black-tailed deer grazing daily across the clearing, and give thanks.

At night, in warm weather, we would camp out on the front porch and stare at the stars until we fell asleep. Sometimes close girl-friends—Diane and her daughter, Skuya; Janelle Swallow and her sister, Marsha Stands (Al's aunties); or their grandmother Bessie and other older woman friends—would spend the night with us and enjoy our view and peacefulness; Pumpkin and Derya both came out at times. Sometimes we wouldn't see or hear from anyone at all for days, but we were content here on our own and free.

I began to understand that my father was right, that our ways of living do shape our future, that our traditional beliefs can be realized still today. We can take personal responsibility and courage and rise above hardship and be good to one another, even in the hardest of times. We can accept and support without being used and abused. Even in my own generation, people could be good-hearted and walk in a good way with each other. We can live as well as survive. Even in my thirties, I was capable of living this type of life no matter what anyone had ever said or done to me.

I began to write songs and stories and to paint again, completing a three-act playscript about my mother's mental illness (*Icicles*). Travis, Vaughan, and I spent time walking, praying, and just being. We sat around the kitchen table together, like Pumpkin and I once did with Dad, to bead, paint, tell stories, remember, and sing. I sewed and made blankets and taught my kids to fish in those hills, to search for familiar roots and plants for tea, to continue adapting by centering on what is natural in the surroundings. It was the first time I found this state of joyful solitude since leaving fieldwork and horses and the first time my own children were old enough to know the strength of true peace of mind.

Later, long after mourning the year, months after putting up a memorial to honor Al, after completing personal recovery, already convinced by Diane, Janelle, and Pumpkin to go on, I decided to go back to school and study writing and art and to find a place for myself within the work as well. We resettled for a time in Kyle, and in the fall of 1991 I began school at the Institute for American Indian Arts in Santa Fe. My children and I eventually settled in a 150-year-old adobe, surrounded by an old irrigation ditch, a river, and red mountains greatly speckled with cedar brush, sharing the place with a Navajo and Shawnee couple (Gino Antonio and Molly Big Knife, also IAIA students) and their newborn (Kaene Eagle). During a night with great thunderstorms high in the desert mountains of Cundiyo, New Mexico, I experienced a sudden awakening after a hard, lucid dream:

> I am an older woman. Older, more complete in life—time-less. A river's current brutally thrashes me, rock to mossy

rock, without ever allowing me time to firmly snag myself in place. I am beaten—drowning or already dead—and can only remember to remind myself on the other side exactly where I have come from, yet it is in a time and place where there are no named addresses or locations, only landmarks and specific descriptives to lead me home.

I awoke standing away from where I'd slept, houseguests screaming because they momentarily saw an old woman standing over them when they opened their eyes.

Today, even after this much of my life has passed, all I know for certain is this: In this river, this strong life current pulls me ever on by its swiftness, dislodges, and sometimes haplessly drowns me; I am always resurfacing no matter how weary, still traveling on.

Now, seven years past living this last entry above, a young deer comes to this cabin's back porch, just now, nibbling green jutting through brightly colored fall leaves. I did leave this work, creeping out and watching her as she relaxes and lies down under the nearby trees. Now I can still see her lying within the wood where she has probably lain many evenings without my knowledge, though I often heard her hooves in the night.

And I know she is fully allowing me to finally distinguish her white tail and black eyes from bark and leaves and watch her fall to sleep, knowing I am nearby; allowing me to be invisible as a human being, knowing I am a carnivore without a weapon, maybe even knowing I'm at peace this particular moment after all these years. I have come to comprehend this certain balance of genuine acceptance and willfulness through loss and through living at this point in my life. Somewhere in this rhythmic motion, I know there is a natural place within the world, within my life, within the work, within surviving and living.

This is me, A lee sa na/E li sa na, from A do he, of Cherokee and Huron mixed-blood and life.

I am done speaking for now.

Singing an Indian Song
A Biography of D'Arcy McNickle
By Dorothy R. Parker

Crashing Thunder
The Autobiography of an American
Indian
Edited by Paul Radin

Turtle Lung Woman's Granddaughter
By Delphine Red Shirt and Lone
Woman

Telling a Good One
The Process of a Native American
Collaborative Biography
By Theodore Rios and Kathleen Mullen
Sands

Sacred Feathers
The Reverend Peter Jones
(Kahkewaquonaby) and the Mississauga
Indians
By Donald B. Smith

Grandmother's Grandchild
My Crow Indian Life
By Alma Hogan Snell
Edited by Becky Matthews
Foreword by Peter Nabokov

Blue Jacket
Warrior of the Shawnees
By John Sugden

I Tell You Now
Autobiographical Essays by Native
American Writers
Edited by Brian Swann and Arnold
Krupat

Postindian Conversations
By Gerald Vizenor and A. Robert Lee

Chainbreaker
The Revolutionary War Memoirs of
Governor Blacksnake
As told to Benjamin Williams
Edited by Thomas S. Abler

Standing in the Light
A Lakota Way of Seeing
By Severt Young Bear and R. D. Theisz

Sarah Winnemucca
By Sally Zanjani

USED